Tea with Arwa

Tea with Arwa

One woman's story of faith, family and finding a home in Australia

ARWA EL MASRI

Author's note: Where I have referred to the Prophet Mohammad within these pages I have not included the saying 'Peace Be Upon Him' after every reference. After each mention of Allah I have not included 'Praise And Glory To Him' after the reference. However, both are in my heart.

Recipe note: I like to use salt in my recipes but suggest you modify the salt you use depending on your taste and medical dietary requirements. I hope you enjoy!

First published in Australia and New Zealand in 2011
by Hachette Australia
(an imprint of Hachette Australia Pty Limited)
Level 17, 207 Kent Street, Sydney NSW 2000
www.hachette.com.au

This edition published in 2012

Copyright © Arwa El Masri 2011, 2012

This book is copyright. Apart from any fair dealing for the purposes of private study, research, criticism or review permitted under the *Copyright Act 1968*, no part may be stored or reproduced by any process without prior written permission. Enquiries should be made to the publisher.

National Library of Australia
Cataloguing-in-Publication data

El Masri, Arwa.
Tea with Arwa / Arwa El Masri.

978 0 7336 2977 8 (pbk.)

Muslim women – Australia – Biography.

305.48697092

Cover and text design by Christabella Designs
Author photograph courtesy of Zeinab Rifai
Sun illustration courtesy of iStockphoto
Other illustrations courtesy of Reem Abousamra
Typeset in 12.7/16.9 pt Adobe Garamond Pro by Bookhouse, Sydney

I dedicate this book to all the women in my life who have shaped me. Grandmothers, mothers, aunts, sisters, daughters and friends who selflessly do what women have done for centuries, support one another.

To my dear husband and friend, Hazem, who is the love of my life. Your love and support in whatever I do is a credit to your manhood. You are a true Muslim gentleman.

And to Lamya, Zayd and Serene – you are eternally a part of my being.

Contents

Recipes		ix
Preface		xi
One	Thursday's Child Has Far To Go	1
Two	'Cucumbers, Cucumbers, Sweet Fresh Cucumbers'	23
Three	A Carpet of Lilac	35
Four	Time Travelling	59
Five	A Different World	87
Six	A Sun-kissed Aussie	121
Seven	The University of Life	141
Eight	The Year of El Magic	159
Nine	A Formal Engagement	189
Ten	Mrs El Masri	203
Eleven	The World Keeps Turning	227
Twelve	From Cedars to Gum Trees	247
Thirteen	A Football Wife	257
Fourteen	Where the Heart is . . .	269
Glossary		297
Acknowledgements		301

Recipes

Mamoul (date-filled biscuits)	19
Kabsa with chicken	21
Bamia (okra and lamb in tomato)	32
Sage tea (Maramiah)	34
Lamingtons	55
Mulberry jam	57
Asmaa's Um Ali (Egyptian dessert)	58
Fatoush salad	77
Falafel	79
Deep-fried Kibbe	81
Palestinian Mansaf Asmaa-style (rice with lamb and cooked yoghurt)	83
Moroccan couscous (with pumpkins)	112
Katayef	114
Yalanji (Warak enab bi-zayt) vegetable-filled vine leaves	116
Moroccan chicken couscous	118
Arwa's pesto paste	120
Aussie pavlova with a hint of Mediterranean topping	138
Foul with tahina	154
Labneh	155
Za'atar	155
Amal's sausage rolls	156
Chicken kebabs	185
Lamb kebabs	186
Arwa's cheese and herb sambousek	187

Dad's Turkish coffee	201
Munazala (mince-stuffed baby eggplants in tomato base)	223
Tabouli salad	225
Dad's favourite orange cake	243
Babaganoush	244
Khubz Arabi (Arab bread)	256
Reem's creamy chicken and mushroom pasta	267
Lamb shoulder and rice Quzi-style	290
Samka Mashwi (oven-baked fish)	293
Cucumber and yoghurt salad	295

Preface

My name is Arwa. I am a proud and happy Muslim Australian woman. If you see me on the street you might think I look mysterious because I wear a veil. Yet the way I live, the way my family and my friends live, is not a mystery. My religion is not a separate room that I visit once or twice and then leave. It is a natural part of everything I do.

It is a way of life. I would like to share with you what it means to me to be a Muslim Australian woman; to share with you my story and the way Australia has given me a place to call home and the opportunity to become the woman I am. To have a country where one belongs is one of the greatest gifts and one that my parents strived to give their children. I was a happy child who always looked for the positives, but it still took me a while to find my place, to settle and then to explore my identity as a woman and a Muslim in Australia. If you were in my home I would pour you a traditional Arabic coffee or a cup of tea and serve you some lamingtons, make you comfortable and share with you my life.

I love food and all its wonders. I love how a dish from a country can tell you so much about the people and the land it comes from. Our senses have a remarkable ability to remember where and when we first smelled or tasted a particular food. Are you like me? My senses go into a frenzy when I see or smell a food that is linked to a special time in my life, be it happy or sad. It's as if I were right back in that moment. Taste and smell can make a memory so vivid that you uncontrollably smile when you eat a meal linked to something good, or push it away if it reminds you of something unpleasant.

Food is a major part of my life and it plays a huge role in bringing my family and extended family together. On a broader scale, I believe it can bring communities together and encourage conversations between people who may think they are very different; eating together and discussing a dish they both enjoy can unite the most unlikely. Eating the foods of other cultures can teach you so much about them. In my eyes eating the food of another country is a personal act of diplomacy.

The old saying 'to break bread together' means something profound to me, because if you share a meal with someone you have shared far more than food; you are sharing a moment in which you stop and sit together, a moment to feed not only the body but also the soul. From then on you are linked – neighbours, friends, work colleagues, brothers and sisters – how beautiful is that?

In these pages I will share with you my life and, in doing that, I will revisit periods in my life, meals and moments with friends and family. It is these small moments that create a rich life. For you to know me, I need to let you into my heart and into my home, share my family stories and my faith. By doing this you will see how similar we are – all looking for safety, love, family and a sense of belonging . . . and a good meal. Here is my past, my present and a hint of my future . . . with a touch of cinnamon in many a dish.

Chapter One

Thursday's Child Has Far To Go

I was born in Riyadh in Saudi Arabia on Thursday, 28 October 1976. I arrived in the early hours of the morning, right before sunrise. In Islam this time of the day is called *Fajr*, and is the time of the first of five obligatory prayers Muslims perform each day. I was obviously eager to make myself known with the call to prayer, 'Allah is great', echoing throughout the city as I arrived. I was an unplanned home birth. Our neighbour, who was thankfully a midwife, was the only medical help my mother had. My mother had been so sure I was going to be a boy, having already given birth to my two elder sisters.

Maha had the novelty of being the first and then four years later Reem was born. Reem had big eyes and long eyelashes and was a gorgeous baby, which helped offset the fact she was a crier who didn't give my mother an easy time. My mother's third pregnancy, carrying me, was different from the two before. She felt lighter and more energetic, with a radiance that people commented on as being youthful. Her steadfast conclusion was she was having a boy, a boy who would carry on the family name, who would be everything she hoped for and a son who would look after her in her old age.

When our neighbour handed me to my mother, well, I think it's fair to say I was lost in translation. A girl! My mother was disappointed that she had been so wrong. At least I was a small and quiet baby and not much trouble at all. I was the third girl in my Palestinian family and the one right before the boy. Don't misunderstand me, my parents loved us girls very much, but once my brother, Firas, was born two and a half years later I could always feel some unconscious favouritism towards him.

The Middle Eastern culture, for reasons unrelated to Islam, favours boys. I am sure that these reasons are similar to any other culture in the world where male dominance is an issue. For centuries women all over the world have had to work hard to gain equality. For instance, in Australia the female right to inheritance was earned only in the early 1900s. Incidentally, Islam introduced these rights more than 1400 years ago. This does not mean that every Muslim male abides by the rules and doesn't wrong a woman, but what it does mean is that the mistakes made are committed by individuals or governments, not by the religion.

Islam teaches that both men and women are equal in the eyes of Allah and the only thing that makes one person, regardless of gender, more enlightened than the other is how committed they are to God, and the goodness and kindness of their heart. Being committed to Allah and staying kind and good are what I strive for and what I believe Islam is about. As a mother today with two girls and a boy I do my best always to be fair and commend them on their actions rather than their gender.

But perhaps my sense of being lost in translation wasn't only to do with my gender. We moved to the United States when I was very young so my father could complete his degree in civil engineering. Firas was born while we were living there, in Tucson, Arizona. We spent two and a half years in the United States and maybe that had an impact on my sense of home. I know it had an impact on my memory because one of my strongest childhood memories is of fear... and pumpkins. It was Halloween Eve in Tucson and I was walking home with my sisters Maha and Reem and our neighbour, Rebecca, with Firas in his stroller. I was almost three. Even now if I close my eyes, I can see the pumpkins with angry faces looking at me. The smell of pumpkins and burning candles filled the air. I was terrified that something we cooked could be so frightening. I didn't eat pumpkin for years after that night.

As he was born there, Firas is the only member of our family with an American passport. This sense of belonging or identity, or lack of it, is part of the reason my father and mother decided they should migrate to Australia. They wanted to give their daughters an identity that would allow us to further our education and have careers if we pleased. Unlike American or Australian law, Saudi Arabian law does not entitle one to the rights of citizenship simply by virtue of being born there. This troubled my father but it would take a few years for him to find a solution.

Besides a fear of pumpkins, the other thing I took back with me to Saudi Arabia was a strong American accent. It would mark me as different and already I was a child of many worlds. I wasn't worried about this at the time. I was too young. It was much later that I started to question where I belonged.

I remember Saudi Arabia well. The landscape is unique, so yellow and dry. The heat and humidity made me feel as though I were in a sauna, and in winter the cold, dry desert air would pierce through my skin. I loved it. As a child I loved the palm trees dotted everywhere, carrying dates so sweet. And it seemed to me that all roads were four-lane highways filled with the latest luxury cars from around the world. Green parks and manmade waterfalls were oases among the desert sands. The shopping centres were fit for a king, with entire shopping complexes selling only gold. You could walk into a three-level shopping centre and *all* they sold was gold!

In Saudi Arabia there is no distinct middle class, you are either rich or poor. The rich are super-rich. My sister Maha once took me with her to visit one of her high school friends, a girl called Huda. I couldn't believe it when we walked into her high-walled mansion compound and found a whole new world within this concrete fence. Huda's house was a four-level mansion with two tennis courts, an indoor heated pool and a car park the size of a small shopping centre. A row of prestige cars crowded the garage, seven in total, and there was a driveway with a drop-off zone right in front of the door. When we walked into the house proper there was a waterfall in the middle of the entrance hall with fish in the pond. The marble stairs and crystal chandeliers were breathtaking and there was a lift that could take ten people. They had their own disco, gym and an entertainment area with billiard tables and there were television screens wherever you looked.

All the curtains were remote controlled, and the kitchen was the size of a small house. The breakfast table seated twenty people, even though there were only five people in Huda's family. Huda asked us 'What do you feel like eating?' We were too shy to say anything. 'How about pizza?' she said. We nodded and she turned to the five maids waiting in the kitchen and said, 'Make us some pizza.' They scrambled and one of them opened the pantry door. It was like a small supermarket with everything you could ever need right there. Within twenty minutes we were eating homemade pizza with all the trimmings! With their fifteen maids and ten cleaners Huda's family were one of the super-rich. I don't know how many gardeners they had or whether each car had a separate chauffeur. The luxury was truly over the top.

The Saudi middle class were mostly the foreigners from other Islamic countries, like us. There was no obvious prejudice against non-Muslims as so many lived and worked in Saudi Arabia. Yet there was a strange duality; the Saudis were incredibly welcoming to foreigners and migrants as long as they had a reason to live there and had proof they were employed. You couldn't purchase property in Saudi Arabia if you weren't Saudi. My parents were unable to buy a home for that reason. Americans got around this regulation by purchasing land as a government or business rather than as a private citizen. They built small cities with high walls that housed only American families working in the country. These compounds weren't built to prevent them from mixing with the Saudi Arabians, Americans were welcome to live anywhere they pleased. I guess the Americans just preferred their own ways rather than the Saudi ways of life and the Saudi Arabian government didn't object.

I remember when my father started working for Aramco, a petroleum company. Saudi Arabia is the oil capital of the world and many government-contracted local and foreign companies created the infrastructure for the small industrial towns built around the oil extraction projects in the middle of the desert. You could not enter the American compounds unless you were authorised. My father had a special pass. He took us for a ride one day into one of them to proudly show us his craftsmanship – we often drove on the roads he was in charge of and he would say, 'Can you feel how smooth that is? No bumps.' I was so proud of him as we floated over the even surface.

In the American compounds you'd think you were in a suburb of the United States. The streets, the shops, even the houses and street signs, were replicas of everything back in America. They had their own cinemas and American products and schools. I remember reading a sign for 'Hot American apple pie' and my father stopping to pick one up from the bakery. The soft cooked apples and buttery crust melted in my mouth. We had eaten apple pie regularly when we lived in the States. I loved it. There was no chance of an American getting homesick in these compounds, it was like a transplanted country. Within a compound the Americans could do what they liked, but when they stepped out of the gates they had to consider Saudi sensibilities and dress modestly, especially the women. Women were not expected to wear a veil but all Westerners were expected to respect Saudi Arabian customs, which meant things like not possessing alcohol or recreational drugs.

For a Muslim, Saudi Arabia is the land of the holy city of Mecca, where the Kaaba stands, an ancient stone cube structure the foundations of which Islam teaches have been there since the beginning of time, and is the centre of the Muslim world. About three hundred or so kilometres from Mecca is the city of Medina where the Prophet Mohammad is buried. The stones of the Kaaba were built by the Prophet Ibrahim; all Muslims face Mecca in prayer. Wherever Muslims are in the world, when they pray they turn to face Mecca. Millions of Muslim pilgrims from around the world set out to visit Mecca every year and have done so for more than 1400 years to perform the duty of Hajj. How wonderful, a wave of cultures so different from one another standing shoulder to shoulder in prayer.

Despite the stable employment and proximity to his family that living in Saudi Arabia gave my father, he did not like the way we were referred to by the Saudis as 'foreigners' even though his three girls had been born there. Nor did I. It didn't matter where you came from, where you were born or what religion you were, you were still a foreigner if your parents were not Saudi. I don't think it was a derogatory reference but even as a young child it still felt odd to hear one Muslim label another a foreigner, since Islam teaches unity regardless of where you come from. I remember being at school and as a *foreigner* I would have to bring in proof of residency to the school inspector every three months. She would walk into the class and interrupt the lesson and say, 'All the foreign girls make sure you bring your papers of residency with you tomorrow.' I hated hearing those words, they made me feel so insecure and to some extent humiliated.

In spite of these strict citizenship rules, migrants are welcome to stay in Saudi Arabia if they have working visas. But most people have a country to go back to, we didn't. I was a second-generation Palestinian who had never seen Palestine because of the Israeli occupation. I still haven't.

The Saudi Arabian government took this position on citizenship because if every Palestinian born outside Palestine were to be given a new identity, the number of Palestinian people would rapidly diminish. It would be an unintentional eradication of a race of people. But for us it meant that my sisters and I did not have a country to call home. The situation seemed to contradict what Islam teaches, a world of unity and kindness.

We were not alone in our predicament; there were many Palestinian families living and working in Saudi Arabia. Like us, they would go to school alongside Saudi children for school was free for all, Saudi and non-Saudi. Publicly funded education for girls began in 1960 under the inspiration of then Crown Prince Faisal and his wife, Iffat.

I enjoyed school, worked hard and was a top student alongside the other foreign girls – Jordanian, Egyptian, Lebanese and Syrian. Maybe I felt I had to prove myself because I looked different, with fair hair and light-coloured eyes. I know it is a generalisation but in my class the Saudi Arabian girls never really seemed interested in studies, they were more focused on who had the better henna in their hair or on their hands. Until we were older we didn't wear the veil at school, that came when we reached Year Five. There was one Saudi Arabian girl who stood out from the rest. She was smart. Her name was Mannel and she had the most beautiful voice – when she recited the Quran my eyes would well up. This was an amazing gift. Mannel was so good she would be asked to recite some passages from the Quran at assembly every morning before the national anthem. This ritual was practised in every school in Saudi Arabia.

In Islam it is obligatory for both men and women to be educated. Although general illiteracy was widespread in the 1980s, this did not apply to knowledge of the Quran. You could go out into the middle of the desert, find a small tribe of Bedouins and ask the sheik to recite anything from the Quran and this would be done with no hesitation. But if you gave him a book he could not read it. Prophet Mohammad was illiterate and the first words revealed to him by the angel Gabriel were 'Read in the name of thy Lord'. The Bedouin live by Islam, it is in the way they eat and in the way they talk, the way they run the family, and how they sit and sleep. It is a beautiful way of life if followed just as the Prophet Mohammad had taught.

When I was a young girl in Saudi Arabia it was still not the norm for women to strive for a career or to achieve a high education, but my parents, especially my mother, had always encouraged us to study and try hard at school. She had been educated and had worked even after her marriage so she was a good role model for her daughters. Things are a lot different in Saudi Arabia today, though there are still some restrictions for women.

In the past twenty years women in Saudi Arabia have excelled in many different fields. Despite the images portrayed by some in the Western media, Saudi Arabian women are increasingly recognised for their achievements. They are managers of multi-billion-dollar companies, world-renowned scientists, university deans, bank CEOs, deputy ministers, and one Saudi woman is a director of the United Nation's Population Fund. Still these women are not allowed to drive; they have to get around this by having a chauffeur to take them wherever they please. This restriction on driving is something I don't understand. It is not forbidden by Islam. In fact, Islam requires every parent to teach their children three fundamental life skills: swimming, so they do not drown; archery, which translates today to self defence; and horse riding, which translates to being mobile. Of course now we don't use horses to get around, instead we drive cars, so a parent should teach their child to drive. Islam as a religion and a way of life is timeless and evolves with modern changes. But this restriction on women shows that the government, not Islamic teaching, has decreed that women should not drive.

Saudi Arabian women are denied many of the rights granted to women in Islam. As I said earlier, some may not realise that many wrongs that are committed in the name of Islam are actually determined by individuals or governments, not by the religion.

After my father had obtained his degree in the United States he got his first job as a civil engineer back in Saudi Arabia, working for a company whose rich Saudi Arabian owner was illiterate. All his staff were foreigners with degrees in engineering, accounting and business and the manual workers were mostly Indian, Filipino or Pakistani. My father worked for this company for many years, and earned his employer's respect for his loyalty and work ethic. Large American companies, like Aramco, had large contracts in Saudi Arabia. It was due to my father's admirable reputation in the industry and his American degree that Aramco subcontracted some major projects to the company he worked for.

With my father's new job, we moved into a ground-level apartment in an average part of Khobar, an oil-rich city on the east coast of Saudi Arabia overlooking the Persian Gulf. My memories of the time are very closely linked to everything I felt and smelled.

The hot desert air would dry out my nose and the heat was sometimes unbearable in the middle of summer; it was normal for my mother to run the air-conditioning unit all day and night. We would leave our air-conditioned home, get in our air-conditioned car and then dash from this to whatever air-conditioned destination we were heading to, be it shopping centre, school or relative's home.

The heat was at times so high I would find it hard to breathe. It was like the hottest summer day in Sydney for weeks on end. In Australia it is called a heatwave, in Saudi Arabia it is called summer. Nobody went out between midday and 2pm. The weather and lifestyle in Saudi Arabia allowed for *Qailulah*, what people in Europe refer to as a siesta period, or rest time, between midday and early afternoon. The Islamic 'siesta' was taught to Muslims by the Prophet Mohammad. Between the midday prayer, *Dhuhr*, and the mid-afternoon prayer, *Asr*, you are encouraged to have some down time as it revitalises and relaxes your nerves and spine, and it also gives you energy for the rest of the day.

The Saudi Arabian working day runs between 7am till midday then from 3pm to 6pm, ending just in time for *Maghrib*, the fourth obligatory prayer at sunset. In the time of *Qailulah* the shops would close, children would come home from school and fathers would travel home for lunch. I always felt that this lifestyle encouraged the family unit to become stronger. I remember my mother sending me to her room to turn on the air-conditioning so the room would be cool for my father to nap comfortably after we had some lunch together.

After my father returned home from work in the evening we would all have dinner together and then we'd set out to the shops or local park. The varied night life in Saudi Arabia is one thing that stands out in my memory; everything is open till late, just after the fifth obligatory prayer of *Isha*. The city comes to life after dark with families visiting relatives, shopping complexes or leisure centres. The night air is cool and restaurants and ice-cream shops are full of people finding relief after a hot desert day. It is not unlike Australia's Thursday-night shopping every day of the week.

One day we were on our way to visit our neighbour Um Sultan to celebrate *Eid*, the festivities Muslims celebrate after Ramadan, the month of fasting, and Hajj, the pilgrimage to Mecca. My sisters and I were so excited as the streets were lit with lanterns and coloured strings of lights, flashing and glistening in the evening sky. The festivities here in Sydney at Christmas remind me very much of *Eid* in Saudi Arabia. We would get dressed up, eat sweets and receive gifts, just like here. My husband and I often stop and enjoy the decorated houses and flashing lights during Christmas and New Year's as a reminder of celebrations we had seen as children during *Eid*.

Tea with Arwa

That day, I was standing at the door in my new dress with my sisters and younger brother Firas. It was very hot so we began to sweat and fidget. My mother turned to lock the door and then unlocked it to run back in to get the *mamoul*, the traditional sweets filled with dates and nuts we had made for our neighbour.

While we were waiting for my mother, Reem and I leant against the edge of a barrel, twisting and turning to annoy each other as impatient children do. We didn't realise that the barrel was stained with black tar that was hot and sticky from the 40-degree heat. When my mother came back carrying a tray of sweets she took one look at us and I could see anger flash across her face as she ordered us back inside. I looked down and saw that my dress and hands were stained with sticky black tar. We had to take off our new celebration clothes, scrub ourselves and then put on ordinary clothes. The white lacy dress I was so excited to wear, identical to my sisters' dresses, was destroyed. I will never forget it.

My early memories of making *mamoul* were from when we visited my mother's family in Syria. My aunts would sit around the dinner table in a well-organised production line. Each would have a job to do. One would roll the mashed dates spiced with cinnamon and cloves, the other would roll the dough and the third would put them together while two more would bake. My grandmother watched over them all closely. Finally, hundreds of these small biscuits would be stacked in big glass jars ready for the upcoming celebrations. The smell of spices would linger in the apartment for days after. I now bake *mamoul* for my children and I like knowing I am sharing something from my childhood, passing on to them their great-grandmother's recipe and the smell and taste of *Eid*, which I hope they will share with their own children one day.

Thursday's Child Has Far To Go

My grandmother came out to Sydney four times to visit us, the last time for my engagement and wedding in 2000. I remember her sitting at my mother's breakfast table in a shaft of sunlight, telling me slowly and carefully the ingredients and the method for *mamoul* while I wrote it all down in a notebook. I have made her *mamoul* every year since then.

That early day in Khobar, my mother had also used my grandmother's recipe and the apartment smelled of cloves and cinnamon. The *mamoul* has a soft, biscuity crust and when you bite into it you get an aniseed kick in your mouth. They are topped with icing sugar and as you eat all the sugar falls off and powders your clothes. I have taught my own children to give themselves a little brush and it's off, just like my mother taught me.

Not long after I ruined that beautiful dress, we moved from that apartment to a better area of Khobar. The building was only for families, a fourth-level double apartment with two front doors! One was for everyday use, the other for when guests arrived. That door took you straight into the formal lounge. The apartment had two bedrooms, so my sisters, brother and I all shared one room while my parents had the other. The rest of the apartment was quite roomy and it had a couple of balconies.

One of the balconies looked out on a dusty empty lot where the tenants would park their cars. On the other side of the lot was another apartment block that was only for single men, mostly Indian and Pakistani, not families. Our washing line was on that balcony so my mother had a long bed sheet permanently hanging on the furthest rung so that we weren't leered at when we hung up the washing. It only came down when we left for Australia.

The other balcony looked on to a desert park, a huge empty space, trimmed with tall and graceful palm trees and filled with fine, powder-like desert sand. When it was windy I would watch mini tornadoes throwing the sand into a frenzy. My mother would tape all around the edges of the windows of our formal lounge so that the sand would not seep in. But some always did. Dusting was a weekly chore.

This park was regularly used for weddings. Overnight, huge tents would be set up for a traditional Saudi Arabian wedding. My siblings and I would watch for hours as the men danced the traditional Saudi Arabian sword dance with a modest sway, decorated horses tapping their hooves in sequence to the beat of the Arab *daf* (handheld frame drum). One of the tents was for the party, the other for the catering. Sometimes the women were nowhere to be seen; my mother would explain that they had the better location of a private reception hall with no expense spared. The groom would have to walk through a room packed with women to join his bride, with only his father and his new father-in-law by his side. How nerve-racking would that be for him? The smell of the traditional Saudi dish *kabsa,* made with cardamom, cinnamon, bay leaves and curry, would fill the air. The smell of cardamom is, for me, the smell of Saudi Arabia. Everywhere you go it's in the food, the coffee and even sweets. It is an expensive spice that matched the extravagant Saudi Arabian lifestyle.

We would watch, captivated, as the wedding took shape. There would be so much food as the hosts catered not only for the guests but for anyone who could smell the food cooking. Surrounding neighbours would have a parcel of food delivered to them and passers-by would be given a share. Hospitality is one of the traits Arabs have been known for over the centuries. I love this and have continued this tradition of sharing. I have a passion for food and when people come to our home I love to feed them. But it is a trait that I have found belongs not only to the Arabs.

Thursday's Child Has Far To Go

The first time I ever tasted *kabsa* I was eight years old. It was made by the wife of my father's boss during a camping trip we went on without my mother, who was visiting her family in Syria. We ended up in the middle of the desert with the entire extended family of my father's boss. We knew no one. A small convoy of tents was set up, all connected to a generator for electricity. These people left the comforts of their mansions to spend a few days in the desert – you can take the Arab out of the desert but you can't take the desert out of the Arab.

The women and children were in a tent separate from the men. Firas stayed with Dad and my sisters and I were shown to the ladies' tent. When we entered, all the women were wearing burqas. They were very nice to us but we couldn't see their faces. The hijab in Islam is obligatory for women and girls who have reached puberty as a girl's body begins to develop and change into adulthood. Hijab means veil which is modest dress and the covering of the hair, neck and chest. Women who wear the burqa do so out of personal choice. It is customary to wear the burqa in Saudi Arabia but there are a lot of women who choose not to. No one in my family wore it. On that day, in the middle of the desert, with wind storms carrying the fine sand at a hundred kilometres an hour, I realised it was sensible for both men and women to cover their faces, otherwise the sand would blind them.

When the food was served it came out on a huge round serving tray. There was a mountain of rice with chunks of lamb so tender they were falling off the bone. Fragrant toasted nuts and raisins were sprinkled on top of the rice. Arabian tradition is to sit on the floor with thin cushions beneath you – there were no chairs or tables in sight.

The food was placed in the middle of the tent on the softest Persian rug. The rug looked and felt expensive. The women surrounded the tray and rolled up their sleeves to begin to eat, revealing arms laden with gold, designer watches and a diamond ring on nearly every finger. I was too young but my sister Maha noticed that sort of thing so was impressed. They all lifted their burqas to eat, revealing a unique Arabian beauty, big eyes lined with black kohl and smooth olive skin with fine Arabian features.

We were so shy and embarrassed as there were no spoons. When I looked over at Maha she was using her fingers, the thumb, pointer and middle fingers in the way of Prophet Mohammad. She was taking a mouthful and eating it. I looked around and everyone was using their hands. Reem and I gave it a go and the rice went everywhere. One of the women looked at Maha and said, 'What's wrong?' Maha looked up and apologetically replied, 'They can't manage, would you have any spoons?' The woman looked at us strangely and called out to the maid to bring her some spoons. I remember other children there, about our age and younger, who managed just fine. Now, as an adult, I understand the look we got from that woman, as if we were city people and they were Bedouins, an unintentional insult, I promise you.

Mamoul (date-filled biscuits)

For this recipe you will need a date mamoul mould, which you can find at any Middle Eastern grocer.

Ingredients for dough

    150ml light sour cream
    250g unsalted butter, melted
    1½ cups fine semolina
    2 cups self-raising flour
    ¼ tsp mahlab (found at any Middle Eastern grocer)
    2 tbs aniseed, lightly bruised in mortar and pestle
    ¼ cup cold water, you may need more water when kneading the dough

Ingredients for date filling

    1kg packet pre-mashed dates, sold at most Middle Eastern grocers
    1 tbs ground cinnamon
    ¼ tsp ground nutmeg
    ¼ tsp ground cloves

Method for dough

Combine all the ingredients except the water and knead until combined. Add water in portions and knead well until dough forms a ball. Do not allow dough to rest, dough is ready to use instantly.

Method for filling

Place the dates in a mixing bowl and add all the spices. With your hands mix well. Lightly oil a tray and your hands with vegetable oil and roll date mixture into balls the size of a small walnut.

Method for mamoul

Preheat your oven to 200°C. Take a small amount of the prepared dough, about the same size as the balls of date mixture you prepared earlier, spread it into the palm of your hand and place the date ball in the middle, then gather the ends of the dough until the date mix is completely covered. Place it in the mould and press down to make a flat surface, turn the mould over and release the biscuit.

Place on a baking sheet and bake for 15 to 20 minutes or until bottom of the biscuits are golden brown. This dough is best when the biscuits do not brown on top. Take the biscuits out of the oven, allow to cool in baking tray for 5 minutes then place in a deep dish and cover with a tea towel. When completely cooled, store in a dry glass biscuit jar with a tight lid to keep them fresh.

Makes approximately 45–50 biscuits.

Kabsa with chicken

Ingredients

- 500g long-grain rice
- 2 tbs butter
- 3 large brown onions, diced
- 3 large tomatoes, diced
- 1 tbs ground cardamom
- 1 tbs mild curry powder
- 1 tsp ground cinnamon
- 1 tsp ground pimento
- ½ tsp ground black pepper
- 1 tbs salt
- 2 dried bay leaves
- 6 tbs tomato paste
- 1 whole chicken cut into eight pieces or 2kg chicken drumsticks with the skin removed
- 1 litre boiling water
- 1 tbs butter for browning the almonds
- ½ cup slivered almonds
- ½ cup sultanas

Method

Place the rice in a bowl and soak in warm water for 20 minutes then drain. In a deep pot melt the butter then add the onions and sauté until translucent. Add the diced tomatoes and cook for 10 minutes while stirring constantly on moderate heat. Then add all the spices and stir to release their aroma for 3 minutes. Add the tomato paste and stir.

Add the chicken pieces and allow them to absorb the colour, seal while stirring continuously for 5 minutes. Add boiling water until all chicken pieces are covered. Cook for 25 minutes or until chicken is falling off the bone.

Remove the cooked chicken and place in a deep dish and cover with foil and a tea towel. Add the rice to the stock and bring to a light simmer.

To ensure you don't have too much stock for the rice stand a spoon in the centre of the rice after it simmers and let go. If it remains standing then the level of stock is fine, if it falls then you have too much stock so you must remove some – a little tip Hindiya taught Mum and she taught me.

Reduce the heat to low, cook for 25 to 30 minutes or until the rice has absorbed all the liquid. Turn off the heat and remove from the stove and cover with a large towel for 15 minutes.

Meanwhile, place the butter in a frypan and melt, then add the almonds and stir constantly until slightly golden. Add the sultanas and stir until they swell up. Then place the rice on to a large communal serving tray, top with chicken pieces, browned almonds and sultanas. Serve with cucumber yoghurt salad.

Serves 6 to 8 people.

Chapter Two
'Cucumbers, Cucumbers, Sweet Fresh Cucumbers'

My mother, Asmaa, is an intelligent and beautiful woman. She is a constant source of strength and support in my life. When I look back at what she has done for our family, and especially for my father, I feel incredibly indebted to her. I wonder at the difference between her childhood dreams and the life she has made. Regardless of how things turned out, I know she is content.

My mother and father met through a mutual friend. My father, Hatem, was a maths and science teacher and my mother taught Arabic and religion. They were both working in a small Saudi Arabian village that had no electricity, just outside Riyadh. My father was a handsome man and my mother says the first time she saw him she thought he looked just like a movie star. Whenever she recounts that first moment I can see her as the young woman she was, with sparkling eyes and an enigmatic smile.

Once they married, my mother still worked and even after the births of Maha and Reem she continued to teach. It wasn't until I was born that it got too difficult and she decided to stay at home. However, my mother didn't give up her teaching skills, she just focused them on us. She would always correct our Arabic pronunciation, try to show us the proper way to do things and answer our questions about the world. These days, I sound a lot like her when I speak to my children. I come from a long line of educated women, my three aunts on my father's side are all teachers as are four more on my mother's side, so in my family there was never any question that girls should be educated.

My mother was the driving force behind my father going to the United States to further his education. The wages of a civil engineer were far higher than those of a teacher so she could see that it made sense for him to consider a career change. They both worked and saved so he could make this life-changing journey to study.

My mother spoke often of how she would have liked to have studied another degree or two in education and maybe have become a school principal or even higher than that. Yet she always put my father and her children first. Whatever hand my mother was dealt she just accepted it and did the absolute best she could. She is what I would call a 'battler'.

I believe my father took advantage of her accepting nature to some extent but, to be fair to him, it is hard not to when you live with someone who always takes on a challenge with a smile and never admits to something being too difficult. My mother was definitely the woman who supported his success. Her support, and the way she put her own dreams on hold so he could fulfil his, meant we all benefitted from her sacrifice. Some years later she would find satisfaction in teaching at TAFE in Australia, but more of that later.

My father left for the United States three months before we joined him there. He had to organise his studies and find us a home.

'Cucumbers, Cucumbers, Sweet Fresh Cucumbers'

It was the summer holidays in Saudi Arabia so we spent those three months with my mother's family in Syria.

My mother was born in Palestine, and was only a few months old when my grandparents were forced to leave because of the Israeli invasion. My father was nearly five years old when he and his parents left, but he remembers Palestine well. His father, Omar, was from a wealthy family. Dad would tell me of the many orange groves they owned. As a child he would run through the rows of trees, pick the fruit and peel it, revealing a sweet and juicy flesh that tantalised his senses. His love for oranges continues to this day and he has an uncanny ability to always choose the sweetest and perfectly ripe fruit.

Syria opened its doors to Palestinian refugees, as did Jordan and Lebanon, however my mother's family believed the rules of residency were more welcoming in Syria so this is where they migrated. My mother says that at no stage in their lives did they feel like strangers, or foreigners, there.

My late grandmother lived in a well-occupied suburb in Damascus called 'the street of the Jews'. This was not a disparaging reference, it was a simple fact that many Jewish families lived there. It was their home. They lived in peace and mutual respect with Muslims and Christians, even after the invasion in Palestine. Arabic and Hebrew were spoken, and neighbours would share coffee and meals and acknowledge each other's religious festivities. Although Syria is predominantly Muslim there were still many Christian Arabs and Jews living there.

My grandmother's name is Hindiya, which means 'the Indian woman'. She was not Indian but it was a name that described the exotic beauty of Indian women who at some time had travelled as far as Syria. They would arrive as part of large travelling groups who would go to the markets of Damascus to sell their exotic herbs and embroidered silks for which they are still renowned today. The name is seen as an expression of beauty rather than identity or ethnicity. How wonderful to describe someone with the beauty of another culture or race.

My grandmother was a young girl when she got married. My grandfather, Ismail, came to her home to ask her father for her hand in marriage; she was only thirteen years old. Marriage in those days was a traditional certainty. To start a family and have children was expected. Around the world and throughout history many marriages were a means of continuance. Marriage was not always for love or compatibility but was a means for families to grow and pass on traditions and heritage. My grandmother always spoke of this, she had never felt a physical attraction to my late grandfather and he was older, nine years her senior.

My grandmother's fourth-storey apartment seemed huge to me as a child. My four aunts and five uncles and their children would, like us, visit during the summer holidays. My grandmother had 13 children in total but two boys and a girl had died as infants. All the aunts, uncles and cousins would find somewhere to sleep and every morning we would wake up to the calls of prayer from the local mosque. 'Allah is great,' the voice would echo across the city. As soon as the prayer was finished the sound of the travelling fruit and vegetable trolleys would fill the air and the men pushing them would begin to call out 'cucumbers, cucumbers, sweet fresh cucumbers' as if you were standing at Flemington Markets on a Saturday morning.

The sellers carried a range of different produce, and you could pick whatever you wanted while you were at home. A bucket tied to a rope would be lowered to the man selling the fruit or vegetables and one of my aunts would call out wanting a kilo or two of whatever we all fancied for lunch that day. The man would weigh it and she would pull the bucket back up. When she was happy with what he had picked for her she would lower the bucket with the money inside. Perfect home delivery.

One of the foods my grandmother always cooked for us when we visited was okra with tomato puree and chunks of tender lamb. There were never any leftovers, no matter how much she made.

I loved my grandmother Hindiya very much. I was lucky she was visiting us in Australia at the time of my engagement and wedding, which were only a few months apart. She would share my room when she stayed and we would talk for hours. She always smelled of aloe vera. She would moisturise her hands and face every time she washed for prayer. I have to admit she had good skin; she never looked her age, she took care of herself and ate healthy food. She loved sage tea and anything green. She knew what every food was good for and for which part of the body. Later in life she had a condition where her blood was clotting, so her natural remedy to help thin her blood was to increase her intake of onions, instead of aspirin, as they had a similar effect.

I was intrigued and asked her where she got her information from. She told me to go to my mother's library and find the book *The Prophetic Medicine*. Everyone in her family had this book and she swore by it as a guide to deal with health problems and to find remedies taught to Muslims by all the prophets. She was a wise woman and it seemed to me everything she said had a larger message. When I married Hazem I started a library in my home full of books for us to read, and one of those books is *The Prophetic Medicine*.

At their home my grandfather Ismail provided her with a library that was wall-to-wall full of books as she never attended school after she married; he didn't want her to feel as though she missed out on learning. I was lucky to see that library when we would visit her in Syria. It was full of books, hundreds of books of literature and poetry, religion and politics. I remember a Bible and a Torah alongside the Holy Quran.

My grandmother was self-educated but if you sat down and spoke with her for any length of time you'd think she had half a dozen degrees to her name. She read widely as she didn't want to be ignorant of what was going on in the world and she wanted to be able to educate her own children. I respected that about her very much. My image of a well-educated and sophisticated woman comes from my mother and grandmother. They taught me the value of an educated woman and mother. The value goes beyond what words can describe. They are the first teacher to the next generation – what a magnificent and immensely important role to have. There is an old Arabic phrase that sums this up: 'An educated man is an educated individual, but an educated woman is an educated society.' The spirit of my grandmother lives on in me and I hope, like her, I can teach my children well.

If I close my eyes I can see my grandmother sitting in a chair by the window, sewing lace on a nightgown she and my mother had just finished sewing, while singing the songs of Fayrouz. Fayrouz to me is like the Barbra Streisand of the Middle East, a Christian Lebanese woman who is loved by millions for her poetry and the unity about which she sings. She sings of the holy land and the green hills, the trees of olive and jasmine flowers, the tragedy of war on the land and the people who live on that land. She sings of love and the changing seasons. Her enchanting voice sings songs of patriotism that don't offend or hurt, but are unifying, hopeful and peaceful. A soft cry in her voice makes you yearn to visit the places she describes. Fayrouz is probably in her seventies today but she has fans from all ages and backgrounds. My grandmother was one of those fans.

'Cucumbers, Cucumbers, Sweet Fresh Cucumbers'

On the night of my engagement to Hazem, my grandmother and I had a very sad conversation. She said, 'I can see in both your eyes a love I never felt. Look after him, he is a good man.' I think my grandmother had a hard life full of children and responsibilities; I don't think she ever felt romance. She had always told me how my grandfather made her feel safe, that he was a good provider, kind and well educated, who respected her and never spoke a bad word or deprived her of anything. Wasn't that real love?

My grandmother outlived my grandfather by thirty-two years, so she was a widow nearly a third of her life. She was eighty-six years old when she passed away in October 2007. Muslims around the world had just finished fasting for the holy month of Ramadan and the three days of *Eid* festivities had begun. My grandmother Hindiya passed away in her sleep at her home in Syria, on the second day of *Eid*. Although it was the same recipe, *mamoul* that year tasted so different.

Bamia (okra and lamb in tomato)

Ingredients

- 1kg frozen okra (small size)
- Sunflower oil to deep-fry the okra
- 2 tbs sunflower oil
- 10 garlic cloves
- 1kg lamb shoulder, trimmed and cut into medium pieces
- 2 tsp salt (or to taste)
- ½ tsp ground black pepper
- ½ tsp ground cinnamon
- ½ tsp ground pimento
- 800ml water
- 400g tomato puree
- 1 tbs tomato paste
- 1 tbs tamarind paste

Method

Defrost the frozen okra then drain any liquid. Heat the sunflower oil and deep-fry the okra in two batches until some golden colour appears on the edges, then place them on paper towels to drain the extra oil.

In the meantime place 2 tablespoons of sunflower oil in a deep pot and fry off the roughly chopped garlic for 1 minute then add the lamb and stir to seal the meat. Add salt, pepper, cinnamon and pimento, stir then add the water, tomato puree and tomato paste. Cover and cook until tender. I like to use a pressure cooker to achieve a much more tender meat in all my dishes and reduce the cooking time.

When lamb is cooked add the okra and tamarind paste and cook until okra is tender. This usually takes 5 to 7 minutes in a pressure cooker. Serve with boiled rice topped with toasted almonds.

Serves 4 to 6 people.

Sage tea (Maramiah)

Ingredients

    1 tsp dried tea leaves or 1 bag of Ceylon tea
    3 dried sage leaves or dried sage stem
    Boiling water
    1 tsp Tasmanian leatherwood honey

Method

Place tea and sage leaves in a small teapot or mug and pour in boiling water and cover with a lid to trap all the goodness. Remove the lid after 5 minutes and stir in the honey. Nature's medicine to an upset stomach.

Chapter Three
A Carpet of Lilac

My mother and father had built a good life in Saudi Arabia but still for my father it was not enough. He needed to know that his daughters could further their education and stand on their own two feet if anything ever happened to him. Like my mother, he believed that a woman should not depend entirely on a man for her existence; he wanted us to be independent. But as long as we were denied a stable residence in Saudi Arabia, this could not be assured. His eyes turned to Australia.

One of my mother's brothers, Mohammad, had told both my parents about living in Australia. Mohammad is a popular name among the Muslim people so you are bound to have three or four men with that name in an extended family. If we were to come to Australia we would need a family member living in Australia to act as a guarantor. This would allow us to work and not ask for assistance from the government. We would need to be self-sufficient while we completed our residency requirements. My father also needed to show he had employment lined up.

Thanks to Mohammad, my parents' savings and a family friend we ticked all these boxes. We had to complete two years' residency within a five-year period to apply for Australian citizenship. My parents decided to travel to Australia, stay for one year, return to Saudi Arabia for three years to earn more money, and then return to finish the one year remaining of our residency. Financially, it was the only way they could make it work until my father found stable employment. He knew he could earn more in Saudi Arabia to cover the relocation and travel costs.

That was my parents' plan, so we all made the four-and-a-half-hour drive to Riyadh to visit the Australian Embassy. I remember walking into the building while my parents explained to us that we would be asked some questions about our English then we'd do a small test.

I was frightened because I didn't know how to read or write English well. Despite being in Year Four, my written English was that of a kindergarten student. In Saudi Arabian schools, English is not introduced until Year Seven, but because of our years in America my whole family could speak some English, though in my mother's case it was limited. My spoken English was fine, partly informed by the free-to-air American channel which aired on Saudi Arabian television, it had shows like *Sesame Street* and *The Cosby Show*. They were our favourite shows to watch after school. I find myself watching these shows with my children here in Sydney and smiling at old memories.

The whole family was taken into an interview room by a tall Australian fellow who broke the ice by offering us some lamingtons. That was the first time any of us had ever tasted that soft sponge cake dipped in chocolate icing and coconut, though it was not the last! When I bit into it all the coconut fell off, luckily onto a plate.

The man spoke to my father about his qualifications in engineering, explaining that this was the main reason why we got the call-back on our application for citizenship. I understood all that was said. After twenty minutes of discussion both Mum and Dad were asked to leave so we could be tested on our English. The man began by asking my sister Maha some questions about her studies; she was in high school at that time and had no problem answering.

Reem was just like me, well spoken in English but unable to read or write in the language. We answered all the verbal questions well, but I wasn't so sure about the written test even though it was pretty basic. There were pictures of shapes: a triangle, rectangle, square and a circle. We had to write the names of each shape. I gave it my best shot but I remember looking at Reem and asking her, 'How do you write this?' Circle sounded to me like it should start with an 'S' so that's what I wrote. I still feel some shame at the mistakes I made on that test. I started to cry because I thought I would be the cause of us not being allowed into Australia.

We went back home to Khobar and within a week my father got the call from the embassy telling him we were successful applicants. We were all excited at the news. Within two months we were packing and ready to leave. My father didn't quit his job, he took three months leave, which was allowed in the terms of a working visa in Saudi Arabia. School had just started so my mother asked our teachers for the textbooks so we could study in Australia in our year away.

At home we covered all the couches with bed sheets so they wouldn't be dusty when we returned. We plugged all the drains, locked all the windows, said goodbye to our neighbours and headed off to the airport. I was worried about missing all my friends at school, my bed and my toys but that didn't last long as the excitement of going to a new place, the land of kangaroos and koalas, took over. We were off on an adventure but little did I know what was waiting for me on the other side of the world.

We touched down in Sydney in the early hours of 24 October 1985, four days before my ninth birthday. Uncle Mohammad greeted us at the airport. It was the first time I had met him. He looked so similar to his brother Osama, who I saw often on visits to Riyadh, so it was a strange sensation meeting him. Uncle Mohammad was born not long after my mother so they had been very close when growing up, but they hadn't seen each other for seven years. When he was seventeen he travelled to England to study computer engineering. He married an Algerian Muslim woman he met there and had his first son in England. My mother paid for his tuition while working in that small village outside Riyadh.

We couldn't all fit into Mohammad's car so my father took Reem and me with him in a taxi. By the time we left the airport it was around the time school children were heading to school. I pressed my face to the window to watch the people on the streets as we drove past. It was a chilly morning and I could see gum trees and the rooftops of closely packed houses. It looked so much like the United States but the smell of eucalyptus in the air was completely unfamiliar. We pulled up at a set of traffic lights and a group of schoolgirls walked past. I was shocked at how short their uniforms were – I could see their knees! And they were walking with boys and some were even holding hands! Reem and I looked at each other with raised eyebrows. In Saudi Arabia our uniforms were ankle-length and the schools were segregated. I remember as a child I was worried I would have to wear and do the same thing. Seeing those school children made me feel uneasy.

We stayed with my uncle and his family for a few weeks before we moved into our own rented home just a few houses away from his. We were enrolled in the same school my cousins went to, Liverpool West Public School, in western Sydney.

When my mother took us to the school to buy our uniforms she ended up buying them two sizes too big so they were long enough to cover our knees. The day I started I was put into Year Four, but I would have to repeat it as the year was so near its end. I walked into the classroom, looking back over my shoulder at my mother longingly, wishing I could go home with her. The class had boys in it, which made me feel uncomfortable. It wasn't as though I had never seen boys before, I had male cousins I played and spent time with, but I had never had to sit so close to a boy I didn't know. Luckily, the teacher sat me beside a girl named Nicola and she was as nice as they come. She was so interested in me and where I came from and from that first day she made me feel better about this new place. She used to help me with my work, but after a few days the teacher realised how behind I was in reading and writing English so I was included in a group of children for separate English as Second Language (ESL) lessons.

There were other migrant children in that class, including Asians, Indians and Islanders. Reem and I were the only Arabic-speaking students in the group. The feeling of being different was hard for me, especially when I was usually so happy by nature. I felt stupid and frustrated because I didn't understand the language. I enjoyed creative writing in Arabic and had been told by previous teachers that I had a natural ability. In Saudi Arabia I was passionate about my story writing and grammar but in Australia the fear of being laughed at or misread was crippling.

I would get a stabbing pain in my chest when the teacher asked me to read.

This was the start of the many anxiety attacks I would suffer during my school and university years. Even though I never talked about my fears or the paralysing physical symptoms that plagued me, I sensed my mother always knew. She would encourage me and tell me it would be alright, and her words gave me some comfort. I realise now that she was probably experiencing similar feelings. She had been an Arabic teacher in Saudi Arabia and now she was struggling to understand and be understood. How isolating and frustrating for her. And what a huge sacrifice she was making for her daughters.

Though there weren't other Arabic-speaking students in my class, there was a small population of Arabic-speaking people living in Liverpool, but not enough to warrant any Middle Eastern grocers. My father and uncle used to drive all the way to Bankstown to buy Arabic bread every week. Just when I was starting to feel more settled, my father came home excited because he had received a job offer from the Department of Main Roads (DMR), a government body. It was in a place called Grafton, in country New South Wales, 630 kilometres north from Sydney and 320 kilometres south from Brisbane.

Once again, my father headed out before us to arrange a home and some furniture. We packed the small things we had brought for our stay and caught the train up to Grafton to meet him. This was my first ever train ride and I remember it vividly. I was mesmerised watching the Australian landscape reveal itself through the glass windows. As we moved away from the urban areas and passed over the sparkling Hawkesbury I couldn't believe the way the bush stretched out for miles. The colour of the land was different, even the shades of green from the trees was a dry green. I was amazed at the size of the trees I saw, trees that were hundreds of years old and that had withstood time and the elements. One tree stood out, it looked like the palms of Saudi Arabia. It was the Cycad, a Jurassic tree that was as old as time. The many bridges and waterways we crossed and then the small towns we flashed through were all so new and so strange. It was so beautifully different to anything I had ever seen before.

We arrived in Grafton in March 1986 and my mother was already three months pregnant with my soon-to-be youngest brother, Mohammad. We moved into a house at 33 Ridge Street, South Grafton, with a paddock at the end of the street and livestock grazing on it. All our neighbours were in their seventies and they were lovely. The woman who lived right next door came over the morning after we arrived to welcome us into the street with a plate of homemade lamingtons (hospitality belongs not only to the Arabs). She was very pleased that some children were going to be living next door. We saw her nearly every day on our way to school and she would say hello, with her tiny bulldog following her wherever she went.

I knew she was a lonely and frail woman. Her children were in their fifties and hardly ever came around to visit so she appreciated having a young family living next door. Most days we'd see her and wave, but some days she wasn't around. Then, not long after we'd moved in, we were woken in the early hours of a cold winter's morning by the sound of a howling dog coming from inside her house. This was no ordinary howl, it sounded like a crying baby. My mother knew something was wrong, she walked over and knocked at the door and waited but there was no answer; she hurried home and told Dad we should call the ambulance. When they arrived they had to break down the door and they found our lovely neighbour dead with her bulldog right beside her. When they brought the bulldog out his eyes were watery and red, he was going to miss his friend.

It was so sad that she had died alone. This was something that showed me a difference between the two countries. Traditionally, the older generation in the Middle East are respected for their knowledge and experience in life and it is just expected that they will be looked after either in their family home or the home of one of their children. It is also a religious responsibility to care for them. Nursing homes are not as common there as they are in the West for this reason. They do exist but mostly for people who have no family to look after them or people who need twenty-four hour medical care. Though Australians may equally respect the knowledge and experience of their elders, it is often from a distance. The dynamics of family differs in the Middle East and Islam teaches that an elderly family member is the responsibility of the children and, if there are none, then the closest chain of family members are religiously obligated to care for them well. This duty does carry a big burden, but it also gives an even bigger reward. The death of our neighbour showed me the different perceptions of the elderly between different cultures.

Reem and I were enrolled into the local public primary school, South Grafton Public school, but Maha, being older, was enrolled in the local Catholic girls' high school. It didn't take us long to make friends with a girl called Katherine, who lived just down the street and was in Maha's class. Her family and ours would become very good friends.

Katherine's house had a huge mulberry tree in the front yard. It was carrying so much fruit that it was falling onto the driveway and staining the concrete. On our way to school one day we passed by Katherine's home and saw the plentiful berries falling off the tree. My mother prompted me to ask why they didn't pick the berries and eat them. Katherine's mother, Annette, said, 'We don't really like them. Do you eat them?' I had to translate for my mother, who didn't speak English well. When Annette learned that we did indeed eat them she said, 'Why don't you bring the kids around this afternoon and pick them all.' And that's what we did. With Annette and Katherine's help, we picked them all.

There are no mulberries in Saudi Arabia but Syria is famous for its boysenberries, which are very similar. These mulberries were bigger and sweeter than any we had eaten there. We all had purple fingers for a week from eating them and my mother made some of them into jam and sent a big jar to Annette and her family to say thank you.

The next morning Annette came around with a plate of scones she had just baked. They were still steaming when we spread the butter and mulberry jam on them. In her other hand Annette was holding a jar of Vegemite, and she encouraged us to taste the Aussie favourite. It was delicious, and like nothing I had tasted before. Since then our pantry has never been without it. Annette just walked through our door and said, 'Put the kettle on, girls!' It is such an Australian thing to do and nowadays I wouldn't give it a thought, but back then we were shocked that a guest would just walk in and ask for coffee in our home. In Middle Eastern tradition this is a big no-no. I do it myself now in the company of close friends.

I instantly felt at home in Grafton, there was such a sense of community, even though there were no other obvious foreigners there. My sister Reem, brother Firas and I were the only migrant children in the whole school. Mrs Wells was my Year Four teacher and she was kind and compassionate and went out of her way to help me with my English. She sat me on the front table right near her desk and she asked a tall, softly spoken girl named Penelope to sit beside me. Mrs Wells bought me special books to help improve my writing. They were Year Two texts and some of the boys laughed at me because of them. They couldn't understand why I sounded American and could speak and understand what they were saying but couldn't read and write.

When all the other children were doing a test Mrs Wells would call me to her side and put her arm around my shoulder to comfort me and say, 'Don't be scared, just do your best.' I would have to read to her some simple words but the whole class could hear my mistakes. When anyone sniggered she would yell at them and put them on detention.

Every week the class got a different spelling list to learn. One of the words on a list was 'blouse' and there was a picture of a blouse. I looked at it and tried to sound out the letters. I thought it was a mistake, could it really be the same word in English as it is in Arabic? I was excited something looked familiar. I turned to Penelope and asked her, 'How do you say this word?' and pointed at it. 'Blouse,' she said. I grinned widely and said, 'We use the same word!' Penelope gave me a smile that was so sincere. It was as if I had just decoded an alien message. The word blouse is used in the Middle East in colloquial Arabic, not formal Arabic. Nevertheless, I was so excited to see something familiar.

I remember wanting to fit in so much at that school and I was forever hiding at lunchtime from a bully boy in my class. He always teased me about my hair and my uniform, which was just below my knees but longer than all the other girls'. When we first started, Reem and I sat alone at lunchtime for weeks before any of the girls asked us to join their group. That boy would giggle

A Carpet of Lilac

and point at me during assembly because I would get most of the national anthem wrong. It hurt to be laughed at but I never stopped trying and joining in that whole year. I wasn't going to let him stop me from smiling. I always found that a smile can crumble the toughest heart; no matter what you have against someone if you see them smiling at you your natural human instinct makes you smile back. And that's how I dealt with all the adversity in my life. I just smiled and tried to fit in the best way I could. Reem was a lot more sensitive, she would be crying for hours about something that happened at school; I remember trying to soothe her many times as she found it more difficult to adjust.

Not long after we had arrived in Grafton Dad had to go back to Saudi Arabia to renew our Saudi Arabian visas because otherwise we would lose them. It was supposed to be for two weeks but when he got there he had a problem with our visa he had to attend to. He left behind his wife, who had little English, a newborn and his four older children in a country town on the other side of the world. This baffled me as a child. From that point on my mother would often have to manage on her own while my father travelled between Saudi Arabia and Australia. A great deal of the time, she was effectively a single parent even though they remain married till this day.

Though I struggle to understand my father's actions I haven't experienced the pressure he was under to keep our residency in Saudi Arabia. It must also have been very hard for him as a migrant in a small country town to find his place with his new workmates. He had to fit in and get along with people who couldn't relate to his experience as a migrant to Australia and who weren't the least bit interested in him, and he had to work for a much younger boss and prove himself all over again. He left a comfortable, well-paid job, an employer who valued him and his experience to come out to Australia for his children's future and stability.

And to turn down a beer at the local pub with his workmates showed he was different. I can see this would be isolating. Islam prohibits the drinking of alcohol as it is seen as an addictive substance that compromises your alertness and ability to function normally, and one that can cause irreparable damage to your health and body. My father would never have attempted to explain why he declined a beer, it would have been just too hard. Sounding as though he was preaching was not my father's way of fitting in. Having a drink after work is a big part of Australian culture, so it wasn't only a religious issue but also a cultural one. He just put his head down and worked hard. He asked Maha one day what 'fair dinkum' meant. She had no idea either. Things like that show how even the smallest things could be puzzling or demanding in a new environment. Having a degree in engineering and speaking formal English was not enough for him to understand it all. I'm sure it would have been very frustrating for him.

Still, for him to leave us alone for such lengths of time was unfair to my mother. We had no car so we would walk to the local shopping centre, which was half an hour away, and carry all our groceries back home. We would each carry a bag or two. It felt like the whole town was watching our procession. We were called 'the new family in town'. My mother had worn the veil in Saudi Arabia and though she made the very personal decision not to in Australia we still stood out. An old lady in the shops heard us speaking together in Arabic one day and turned to my mother and said, 'Are you speaking the overseas language?'

My mother did the best she could but there were a few things she wouldn't do. She never liked eating sliced bread so whenever my uncle came to visit from Sydney he would bring twenty bags of Arabic bread with him. My mother would freeze it, and after ten minutes out of the fridge it would be soft again. The smell of it warming over the flame of our stove was as if it had just been baked, it was a small and delicious reminder of home for all of us.

In August 1986 my mother gave birth to Mohammad and two weeks later my father was off again. As the oldest girls, it was up to Maha and Reem to help my mother. Sometimes that responsibility was too much. Once on our way home from school, Reem was holding Firas's hand when he let go and ran across the road away from her. He was hit by a car and thrown over to the other side of the street. We stood in horror and watched it happen. I thought he was dead. Reem stayed with Firas while I ran home to get my mother. She took one look at me and could see in my eyes something terrible had happened. It must have been terrifying for her. She started crying and ran out after me with Mohammad on her arm. When we got to Firas, she knelt down. He was groaning in pain as he had broken his leg but, thankfully, he was alive. Other people rushed to help and an ambulance came to take him to hospital. His leg was in a cast for weeks. I know Reem always felt guilty about that day and it deepened a sibling rivalry between her and Firas. I knew it wasn't her fault. We were all just children and, sadly, tragic accidents like this happen all the time. We were just lucky that Firas wasn't more severely injured.

I was a happy child and always tried to find the positive in things, as is my nature. I often found myself mediating the numerous arguments between Reem and Firas. I think it was due to that uncontrollable favouritism I mentioned towards the son. I could always see the two sides to any argument and would try and smooth the waters. It didn't always work but sometimes I could make a difference. With all this, and the drama of Firas's accident, my father still didn't come back to Australia.

Grafton is world famous for the prolific jacaranda trees that line its streets. Each year the city puts on Australia's longest running floral festival to celebrate the vibrant lilac flowers that colour everywhere you look. The Jacaranda Festival began in 1934. Trees many metres high are full of these soft bell-shaped lilac flowers and walking down the street when they are flowering is like walking in a flower-lined tunnel. Beneath your feet the fallen flowers create a soft carpet of purple. It is so beautiful to look at that the image has never left my memory. I think my love for the colour purple began with Grafton's jacaranda flowers.

In October 1986 Reem and I were part of the festival. All the local schools perform songs and dance in the town centre. I remember how excited I was. Today when my husband and I drive around the suburbs of Sydney we play a game with our three children called 'spot the Jacaranda tree'. They can't believe how many there are hiding among the other trees. They only stand out from the rest when they flower. Just like a hidden treasure that is always right before your eyes you only see it if you pay close enough attention.

As our year in Australia was coming to an end I celebrated my tenth birthday. Annette and Katherine came to our house for a small party and it coincided with the start of the festival so it almost felt like the whole town was helping to celebrate my birthday. My mother bought a cake and made an Egyptian sweet called *Um Ali*, sheets of golden puff pastry sprinkled with pistachio nuts and sugar, drizzled with milk and cream. It is a favourite during Ramadan. Annette said she had never tasted anything so soft and creamy, she asked my mother for the recipe instantly.

We were going back to Saudi Arabia in four weeks and when Annette found out that my father couldn't come back from Saudi Arabia to help she automatically asked what she could do. It was something a family member would ask and my mother was touched, Annette was her non-Muslim sister in a foreign land. She went out of her way to honour her words by hiring a trailer that we stacked with all our belongings and by driving us back down to Sydney. Annette was a big woman with a big heart, an example of true Australian honour and kindness. From that moment 'mateship' was a term I understood well.

We left Australia in December 1986, just before the end of the school year. I had met some lovely people in Grafton and I will never forget the way Mrs Wells stuck up for me. When I left she gave me the book *Blinky Bill* and said, 'I am sure one day you will be able to read this to your family. Just keep trying.' What a wonderful teacher she was.

I had just finished Year Four, or so I thought. When we arrived back in Saudi Arabia it was only the middle of their school year. The Islamic calendar follows the Lunar year, which means that it follows the cycle of the moon, unlike the Western Gregorian calendar. This is why Ramadan and Hajj shift by roughly two weeks every year and why the school year is different to that in the West. All my friends were in Year Five but the school wouldn't acknowledge my completion of Year Four in Australia so I needed to be tested to see if I was able to join Year Four in the middle of the year. Every day in Grafton we would come home from school and rest for an hour before our mother sent us to our rooms to study our Arabic books. I hated it at the time and complained that it was hard enough to have to learn a new language without then having to switch back to Arabic, but we were definitely blessed that my mother was adamant we keep our Arabic at a high standard.

Being bilingual is an advantage, no matter what two languages you can speak. Today, I teach my children formal Arabic at home rather than speaking in slang. Arabic is the language of the Quran so it is a Muslim mother's duty to teach her children Arabic so they can read it as children and later as adults. The Quran has been translated into many different languages and, as I have read it in both English and Arabic, I can see some things are truly lost in translation. It is now my duty to teach my children.

I did not immediately settle in when we got to Saudi Arabia. I was even more a child of two worlds now and I didn't realise that it would take me years to find my place. I have learned that language is so complex and powerful, but it can be hard to absorb a new language as you get older. I was lucky to become bilingual when I was young. I often find myself thinking in two languages at the same time or starting a sentence in Arabic and completing the other half in English. It sounds strange but everything I say is understandable and makes sense. Like my mother, though, I believe that the true essence and correctness of each language should stand alone and not become a mixture of the two, which creates a broken English and Arabic. The original language should not be lost. I think one of the reasons many migrants struggle to adjust to a new home is because they have to think in two languages and be able to communicate in one or the other. It is also so easy to have your meaning limited and misconstrued if you are not aware of the nuances and idiom or slang of the new language. My mother always told me, 'Make sure when you speak that what you say is correct from your knowledge, facts and pronunciation so people listening understand you.' I try!

A Carpet of Lilac

The move to Australia would have been very hard for my mother as she had always prided herself on being well educated and well spoken in Arabic. When she arrived in Australia that competence disappeared. She didn't speak English well and didn't understand many of the Australian terms and ways, like being called 'love' when she paid for her bus fare. She thought the driver was hitting on her and we had to walk to the shops for months until someone explained that the idiomatic expression wasn't rudeness or a flirtation. The loss of her self-confidence and dignity was irreparable. Although her English has improved significantly over the years, she is always nervous and red-faced if she has to speak to someone in English in the presence of her children.

For my husband and I, English is our second language, but for our three Australian-born children English is their first language. I was determined they would not face the same difficulties I had growing up. My spelling has never been perfect and I didn't want my children to suffer and struggle the same way. They are born here and, in my opinion, they are obliged to learn the language of their country and be excellent at it. But that does not mean they can't learn Arabic too, and be excellent at that as well, or indeed any other language they are interested in.

As Muslim parents my husband and I want our children to learn Arabic and to retain some of our heritage as migrants to this beautiful country. The Arabic language is so rich, expressive and poetic I want my children to experience it and for it to be a part of their identity. I want them to be able to read the Quran in its original text. There are many Muslims from different nations around the world who speak in many different languages but they remarkably can still read the Quran in its original Arabic text. It amazes me that I can walk through Mecca during the pilgrimage and see people from all around the world, dressed differently, talking differently but during prayer they stand shoulder to shoulder and are unified by Islam. Black, white, tall or short, man, woman, Asian, Indian, businessman or farmer, they all stand before God as equals.

Islam teaches that there is no difference between a person who is Arab and a person who is a non-Arab, the only thing that separates them is their *taqwa,* which means their consciousness of Allah. This is why racism and prejudice do not exist under Islam as nothing about a person makes them better than another, it's all about your soul.

Lamingtons

Ingredients

Some melted butter for greasing
½ cup self-raising flour
½ cup plain flour
½ cup cornflour
6 eggs at room temperature
1 cup caster sugar
1 tbs boiling water
2 cups desiccated coconut

Chocolate icing

2 cups icing sugar mix
⅓ cup cocoa powder
¼ cup milk
¼ cup boiling water

Method

Preheat oven to 160°C. Brush a 19 × 29cm (base measurement) lamington pan with melted butter to lightly grease. Line the base and sides with non-stick baking paper, allowing it to overhang slightly. Sift the combined flours together into a large bowl. Repeat twice.

Use an electric beater to whisk the eggs in a large clean, dry bowl until thick and pale. Gradually add the sugar, 1 tbs at a time, whisking well after each addition until mixture is thick and sugar dissolves.

Sift the combined flours over the egg mixture. Pour the boiling water down the side of the bowl. Use a large metal spoon to gently fold until just combined. Pour mixture into the prepared pan and use the back of a spoon to smooth the surface. Bake in oven for 20 minutes or until a skewer inserted into the centre comes out clean. Turn cake onto a wire rack, cover with a clean tea towel and set aside overnight to cool.

Trim the edges of the cake and cut into 15 squares. Spread the coconut over a plate. To make the chocolate icing, sift the icing sugar and cocoa powder into a medium bowl. Add the milk and water and stir until smooth.

Use 2 forks to dip each cake square into the warm icing to evenly coat. Allow any excess icing to drip off. Use your fingers to roll the cake in the coconut to evenly coat, then place on a wire rack. Repeat with the remaining cake squares, icing and coconut. Set aside for 1 hour or until icing sets.

Makes 15 lamingtons.

Mulberry jam

This recipe will work for many fruits that can be made into jam. I have used it with apricots, strawberries, plums, grapes and mulberries.

Ingredients

1 kg mulberries
½ kg white sugar

Method

Wash the fruit well and de-seed the fruit if using apricots or plums. Place the fruit in a large pot with the sugar and place on medium heat, while mixing gently to avoid the mix sticking. When the fruit begins to release some juice the sugar will begin to dissolve. When it has completely dissolved turn down the heat to leave it at a gentle simmer for approximately 1 hour. If the jam is still a bit runny, depending on how juicy the fruits are, simmer for an extra half an hour.

Take the jam off the heat and allow to cool overnight in the pot, covered, then place jam in sterilised jars and store in the fridge.

For a sundried flavour with the apricot jam, place the jam on a stainless steel tray and cover with a piece of cheesecloth (muslin), making sure it's not touching the surface of the jam. Place in a dry spot under the hot sun for two days then taste the sunny difference. Apricot and plum jam can be drizzled with a little extra virgin olive oil and eaten with Arabic bread when served for a true Middle Eastern taste, my father's favourite.

Asmaa's Um Ali (Egyptian dessert)

Ingredients

    2 sheets of puff pastry
    1 cup sugar
    ¼ cup orange blossom water
    2 cups milk
    600ml thickened cream
    ½ cup crushed pistachio nuts

Method

Bake the puff pastry sheets on an oven tray until golden brown in an oven at 180°C. Tear the first sheet of cooked pastry into large pieces covering the base of a deep serving dish. Sprinkle half the quantity of sugar, orange blossom water and milk over the pastry. Repeat the process with the second sheet of pastry then cover with the cream and top with the pistachio nuts. Refrigerate for 2 hours and serve cold. This is my mother's favourite dessert, to be enjoyed after a long day of fasting.

Chapter Four

Time Travelling

This will sound strange to most Australians, but when we left Sydney it was 1986, and when we landed in Saudi Arabia it was 1407 in the Islamic calendar; it was like travelling back in time. There is a very logical reason for the difference. The Islamic calendar uses the timeline of the Prophet Mohammad's migration from Mecca to Medina, the year of his migration is the first in the Hijri calendar, which means 'migration'. It might have been the 1400s in Riyadh, but the technology and lifestyle was definitely twentieth century.

We arrived back in Saudi Arabia in the afternoon, and as we stepped out of the airport it was so cold we needed to put our jackets on straightaway. We'd left the hot Australian summer and returned to a desert winter that was as cold as they come. At least I knew what to expect, as the seasons in Saudi Arabia are far more predictable. In winter it is cold and in summer it is hot. Easy. Back in Australia we had the confusion of nature doing whatever it likes regardless of the season. In Grafton, I'd go to school with a jumper on and by lunchtime it would get so hot and humid I'd wish I was at the beach. A few hours later, when the bell rang to go home, it would suddenly start pouring with rain and then, just as suddenly, the sun would come out and it would be spring again. A song I love by Crowded House called 'Four Seasons in One Day' perfectly represents the Australian weather and its fickle beauty.

My father was there to meet us and as soon as we stepped out of the airport the unforgettable smell of cardamom hit me. But there was another strong scent as well – musk. Saudi Arabians burn it as incense and men wear it as cologne because it was a favourite of the Prophet Mohammad, so the aroma is heavy in the air. As my father drove us home I looked out the window, at places and people that looked so sweetly familiar. I thought of all my friends in Australia and how much I was going to miss them and I wondered if the friends I'd left behind in Saudi Arabia twelve months earlier would remember me.

When we opened the door to our apartment all my things were as I had left them. My bed and toys, my clothes and books, they were all there waiting for me. A flood of emotions went through me, feelings of belonging and memories of moments with the people I love. I was home: this was a culture I knew, a way of life with which I was familiar. A beautiful sound penetrated the walls – the evening call to prayer – something I hadn't heard for a long time. We prayed in Australia but there is nothing like the graceful, harmonious call to prayer echoing throughout the city, calling people wherever they are, whatever they are doing, to stop and walk into the mosque and pray.

Prayer in Islam is not only a spiritual ritual, it is a time to separate yourself from the worldly things that occupy your mind and time, you are connecting with God five times a day in a meditation to clear your mind and revitalise your soul. When you are in a mosque you are in God's house of prayer. It is preferred that men make an effort to congregate in prayer as much as they can, but they are not obliged to do so and many pray at home or in a park or in any clean place. Islam teaches that in the absence of a mosque Muslims are permitted to perform their prayers in any place of worship, such as synagogues and churches, so long as there are no statues. This is because Muslims pray to an unseen God that is all around us, not to symbols of him.

This is not the case for the Friday midday prayer, however, which is obligatory to be performed in a congregation at the mosque as a sermon is delivered by the imam, a leader in prayer. For Muslims, the Friday prayer is the equivalent to a Catholic Sunday mass at church. This is also the case for *Eid* prayers, which are performed on the morning of the first day of *Eid*. And women may pray either in a mosque or at home, as they choose. This is another one of Islam's concessions to women.

There was a mosque at the end of our street and I went there often with my parents. There were many mosques in Saudi Arabia, just as there are many churches in Australia. My father would go to the mosque as often as he could or he would lead the prayer at home with all of us joining in. We even had a mosque at school where the whole school would pray in congregation at midday. Mosques in Saudi Arabia are magnificent, they are grand buildings yet not over the top. At university I researched Islamic architecture in mosques over the ages and learned how each culture is reflected in its designs. I discovered that it is considered Gothic art in the Western world. I was truly surprised. Gothic art is a term that is used in the art world to describe an era that was largely considered art of the middle ages.

Decoration is highly prized in mosques. Not only are gold and silver used; but an array of colours reflect individual cultures of the people. For example, some mosques in Malaysia are lushly decorative, reflecting the culture of Malaysian people. They are so beautifully different.

That night we all sat down to a welcome home dinner that my father bought. It was our family favourite, falafel. This crunchy vegetarian semi-flat ball of chickpeas fried in hot oil is delicious. The balls should be brown on the outside but green on the inside from the parsley used in the mix. The smell of coriander and cumin erupt when you break it in half. We would dip it in tahina, which was thinned with lemon juice, water and a dash of salt. Falafel is one of the best-known Middle Eastern dishes and all the Middle Eastern countries – from Egypt to Iran to Turkey to Yemen – all claim it as their own. I was curious about this so looked it up and it seems it originated from Egypt and was supposedly a food of the pharaohs. There are many variations of falafel and simply changing one or two spices or ingredients makes the taste quite different. I suppose that explains each country's claim to it and also why eating a Lebanese falafel is completely unlike eating an Egyptian one.

Even though we were home we weren't supposed to unpack everything because we would be leaving again. I visited my boxes often to take out a few more things each time without telling my mother. After a week, we were allowed to join school; it was halfway through the year, so all that study had paid off. But there was still a sting in the tail because I was made to start in Year Four again, despite completing this in Australia. All my friends were a year above me and they looked down on me because I was repeating the year. For a proud student, this was painful. This place that I thought was my home, where I spoke the language, and with people who were my friends, made me feel I wasn't good enough. I was smarter than most of the class, I had the reports to prove it, but it didn't matter. I had to start all over again.

Time Travelling

It didn't take long and we all settled back into our routines. But something was changed. I was still the same happy child who worked hard and tried to please my parents, but a little bit of Australia had worked its way into my heart. I missed my Grafton school friends and Mrs Wells.

By the end of the following year it wasn't just my mind that was different. I reached puberty much sooner than my older sisters and I was frightened when I called my mother to my room in a panic. Even though I had learned about some of these physical changes at school, still I wasn't prepared when the changes happened to me! My mother gently explained what was going on, that it was all perfectly natural and calmed me down. I was embarrassed and made her promise not to tell Dad. She agreed and then walked out and went straight into her room and told him. I heard the whole thing. I couldn't believe that my own mother had betrayed my trust! I was outraged and, as a child, I could not understand why she did that.

I didn't confide in my mother much after that and I am sure she sensed a wall between us. I didn't tell her how I felt and how that moment affected me until I had my first child. She was totally unaware of how much she had hurt me. When she knew, she then understood why I never came to her with a secret. But maturity and marriage have mended whatever distance that moment created between us. Now I understand. As a mother I would do exactly the same thing, but I would be careful and discreet.

According to Saudi Arabian custom, now that I had reached puberty I was religiously required to wear a veil. It was a simple fabric wrap that went around my hair and tucked in at the cheek. I liked it. It made me feel mature. I wouldn't wear it when I was out with my family on the weekend, only as a part of my school uniform. Maha and Mum were the only ones who wore the veil.

My parents didn't want me to wear it yet, which confused me. It seemed to me that the guidelines in Islam are clear.

I was also obliged to fast during Ramadan and pray regularly. I was already doing so. Most parents help their children in these Islamic duties by encouraging them to fast and pray. With most children wanting to be like their mum or dad this was an easy transition. When a woman is menstruating, amongst other things, she is not required to perform her daily prayers or fast on those days. This is out of consideration to what a woman experiences during this time, another one of Islam's concessions to women.

I knew all the rules and obligations; religion was, and still is, a main component of the school curriculum in Saudi Arabia. At school I studied six subjects of religion, in addition to maths, science, art, Arabic language, grammar and creative writing. When I finished Year Six I had a foundation in religion that exceeded many adults I would meet in Australia. I consider that a great privilege. When we moved back to Australia I could hold a conversation with people older than me who found my knowledge of Islam remarkably detailed for my age. I would find myself precociously correcting adults in conversations about religion. I was proud of my knowledge and happy to share.

With my mind maturing and craving knowledge I began to question who I was and where I came from. I was born in Saudi Arabia but I could not claim it as my home. My parents were born in Palestine but they could not live there. My parents never taught us to hate anyone but some of the images that I would see on the news about what was happening in Palestine were beyond any explanation and I found them confronting and confusing. Images of the war between Israel and the Palestinian people were on the news in Saudi Arabia every night. One piece of footage that horrified me became imbedded in my mind and it gave me

Time Travelling

recurring nightmares. Israeli soldiers had caught some young boys who'd been standing on a rocky hill throwing stones at the soldiers and tanks. These boys were bound with their hands at the back of their necks and then the soldiers smashed their elbows with a baton, breaking their joints. I couldn't understand why this happened or, why things were the way they were.

Before we returned to Sydney we went to visit my father's family, who lived in Jeddah on the west coast of Saudi Arabia, only thirty minutes by car from Mecca and about five hours from Medina. We didn't see them as often as we did my mother's family but I remember feeling right at home in my grandmother Amira's house. My grandmother had nine children and my father, Hatem, was her eldest child. My mother used to tell me I looked just like my grandmother Amira and when I was older and saw photographs of us I had to agree.

During our visit the entire family filled her small home. My cousins and I played in the courtyard as my grandmother cooked the Palestinian dish *Mansaf*. *Mansaf* is an old traditional Arab dish, its simple ingredients are available in any home so are perfect for when you get that surprise visitor. Amira boiled the lamb neck and lamb pieces in a stock of herbs and onions until the lamb melted, then she would cook the yoghurt and add the meat to it. She would lay the lamb on top of the rice and sprinkle it all with toasted almonds and pine nuts. That spoonful of lamb and rice, dripping with hot yoghurt, is soul food for any Arab away from home. *Mansaf* can be traced back to the time of the early Arab Bedouins and is made in many countries in the Middle East with variations in each country. Whenever I eat it my mind rushes back to that last family visit to see Amira. Eating *Mansaf* also reminds me how we all performed an out-of-Hajj season pilgrimage to Mecca called *Umrah*. That was the first time I had visited this holy land and seen the Kaaba in person. I started to walk inside the high walls of the magnificent Haram or sacred place. The pillars of the three-level mosque were majestic; I was overwhelmed at its size and beauty. When I turned back I could see the Kaaba; it was so huge and perfect. At that stage the government had not yet fibreglassed the building to protect it so the original stone was exposed. The black cover that bears the verses from the Quran in gold embroidery was lifted just a little. There were only a few hundred people there as it wasn't prayer time, so I had time to stare and take it all in.

We stopped to make *wudu*, the washing before prayer, and though we were barefoot the hot sun hadn't heated the tiles on the floor. I was curious and asked my mother about it. She explained about the built-in cooling system that prevents the tiles from becoming too hot for people to walk on. This was important as you must be barefoot to enter a mosque.

There were thirty taps lined up and people were drinking out of cups that were provided and then everywhere I looked there were hundreds more taps. This was the prolific Zamzam water I had learned about in school – the well of water that God created in the middle of the desert for Hagar and her son Ismail, son of the Prophet Ibrahim.

Even today the source of the water astonishes scientists as the well has never dried out, unlike most of the other wells in Mecca. How old it must be! And with such ample supplies it has remained active in the desert since the days of Prophet Ibrahim. I drank Zamzam water in Mecca during that visit and it has a most unique taste and no matter how much you have you can't

Time Travelling

get enough. It quenches your thirst instantly and seems to also give you strength.

I shared my first walk circling the Kaaba with my family, my eyes wide open in wonder. The 'Black Stone' which is on the south-east corner of the Kaaba signifies the place where a person starts and finishes their Tawaf (circling the Kaaba). Set in silver, Muslims believe that it is the oldest stone on earth and that it was sent from the heavens by God. I have read that its elements resemble no other stone on earth. Even though there were not thousands of worshippers there it was still crowded enough that we were pushed back, but I was small and quick and so I grabbed Reem's hand and we squeezed our way through the crowd of women all trying to get a touch of the stone. It felt so smooth and silky for a piece of hard stone and it was such a strange sensation when I felt it against my skin. I had a special bond with Reem as a child as we did so many memorable things together and touching the Black Stone was one of them.

We all had to return to Australia to complete our residency within the five-year time limit. After such a moving pilgrimage, and after visiting his family, it must have been very difficult for my father to pack up and travel so far away to Australia. So, too, for my mother but at least she had her brother there. I understood why we were going but I wasn't thrilled about it. I had just finished Year Six and now I was expected to start Year Seven in Australia. It wasn't enough to have the rollercoaster of a changing body and mind, but I was going to have to deal with this in a different country from the one I thought of as home. To make matters worse, we weren't even going back to Grafton so I had to start all over in a new place. At that stage we were planning to return to Saudi Arabia after twelve months so I knew that any friendships I formed would have a time limit. It wasn't the ideal way to head into high school.

We arrived in Sydney for the second time in August 1989. My grandmother Hindiya came with us to help my mother settle in and to visit her son Mohammad, who she hadn't seen for a few years. After staying with Uncle Mohammad for a few weeks my father found us the perfect home only ten minutes away. We moved into a house two streets away from Liverpool Council, the place where we would eventually be handed our citizenship papers.

The house had belonged to an Eastern European man who left it to his sons when he died. The garden was filled with fruit trees. He had planted nectarines, which carried the most fragrant fruit, and grapevines for his winemaking, and fig and apricot trees full of fruit. The house even had its own cellar. A huge pomegranate tree that carried the fruit of our homeland grew at the entrance of the garden.

Pomegranates are used in so many different dishes in the Middle East, from *fatoush* salad to *kibbe* and *Lahm bi Ajeen* and lots more. The fruit is eaten fresh and is unique, with a hard skin and rosy rubies on the inside that are both sweet and sour. A type of molasses is also extracted from this heavenly fruit and its healing qualities have recently been tested for sufferers of heart disease, cancer and diabetes.

Pomegranate juice is a common drink at many Middle Eastern dinner tables and the fruit is used in sweet and savoury foods throughout the Middle East. The fruit looks so uninviting to eat but as soon as I cut the flesh open and see the beauty of the inside I can't get enough of them in my mouth. I call it a jewel tree.

Time Travelling

At the time we didn't know why this well-kept, lovely home only a fifteen-minute walk from town was so cheap to rent. There was a reason. It turned out that on a sunny Sydney afternoon the previous owner's son-in-law, who had lived next door, fought with his wife. She gathered her children and ran to her parents' home to get away from his drunken rage. He then stormed over to get her, knocked on the door and his mother-in-law answered. The man asked to see his wife and was told she didn't want to see him. That was all it took, he raised the shotgun he was hiding behind his back and shot his mother-in-law in the doorway before stepping over her dead body, walking into the living room and shooting his father-in-law.

The man's wife ran out into a back granny flat with their children and locked the door. She and the children hid under the furniture. He kept shooting at the windows until he ran out of bullets. The woman and her children survived. The murderer called a cab and went to the police station to give himself up. His wife buried her parents and then moved away with the children. He was sentenced to life in prison.

We weren't allowed to use that vacant granny flat but there was a bullet hole in one of the windows. They never replaced it. Until we heard about the history of the house we always wondered what could make a hole with such precision. We lived in that house for six and a half years and only when we were moving out, because my parents had bought their own home, did the owner tell us the story. We stood there horrified as he told us the details of his parents' murder. All those unexplained footsteps and strange happenings now made sense to me! Maybe we were in something else's presence.

The school year was more than halfway through when we returned to Australia. My parents enrolled us in an intensive

English course at Busby High for new migrant teens to help them with language difficulties before they entered mainstream school. Busby High was one of western Sydney's most disadvantaged schools at the time. Reem and I were in a class with girls and boys of all ages who had English problems. We were part of a group of six children who had just arrived from another country. We were all quiet and didn't say much at all.

Many of the kids were loud and disobedient; some would say words to the teacher in other languages that wouldn't sound kind at all. Some would turn their backs and pay no attention. The room where classes were held was stuffy and cramped with too many students: pimply, sweaty teenagers who didn't want to be there.

I was stunned that they were allowed to stay in the classroom and weren't punished for their bad behaviour. I wasn't used to this sort of environment; all the students in my Saudi Arabian class were well mannered and would be strictly dealt with if they even forgot to do their homework. I couldn't believe that the teacher was spoken to here with such disrespect and was completely disobeyed. It was as if the kids were in control. Now I understand the issues of underfunding for programs like this, and the lack of support for teachers and students in this exhausting situation, but at that time I was shocked by this behaviour that was completely foreign to me.

Because I had matured early, a few boys started to look at me, showing off to try to get my attention. I didn't understand their behaviour. I was so innocent and had no idea of the meaning behind some of the disgusting things they'd say – but I knew it was rude. Reem would stick up for me and try to protect me, but then they would start hassling her as well.

Thankfully the Christmas school holidays began and my days in that hot, overcrowded classroom ended. The short time I spent

Time Travelling

there did improve my writing and reading but it wasn't enough to ease my worry about high school. My father decided to use the holidays to show us the beauty of Australia.

The first time we set out from Liverpool train station and arrived fifty minutes later at Circular Quay in the heart of the city, I was so excited. We got off the train, then lined up to buy tickets for the ferry. It was the first time I had ever been on a big boat. The sight of the blue harbour was breathtaking and I didn't know where to look with the Harbour Bridge, the Opera House, Fort Denison and all the boats bustling about on the water. The smell of the sea and the ocean spray hitting my face was exhilarating and the smell of the salty ocean filled the air.

We stepped off at Manly Wharf and headed down the pedestrian Corso to the beach. From a distance I could see the coastline and the yellow sand meeting the deep blue sea. It looked a little like the beach in Saudi Arabia until we got close and I saw the nearly naked bodies lying on the sand. I blushed. I heard someone say 'G'day' to my father. At first I thought he knew them but he didn't; the people at Manly were just so welcoming.

We sat and watched surfers catching wave after wave and then I spent hours playing in the sand. My mother and grandmother walked down to the water's edge and lifted their dresses just high enough so the waves wet them up to their knees. Time flew by and only when we got hungry did we get distracted. Dad headed off to the shops and he came back with a stack of boxes filled with the classic Aussie beach food – fish and chips.

Is there anything more perfect to eat when you are at the beach and starving? The boxes were steaming as he opened them and the battered fish was so soft on the inside once I cracked through the crunchy case. A squeeze of lemon and a dip in tartar sauce made it taste even better. My grandmother picked up a bit of fish and just looked at it. It was like nothing she had ever eaten before. What the Australians call hot chips and tomato sauce we knew as French fries and ketchup, but the Australian version was sprinkled with chicken salt and so thick and crunchy yet nearly boiled on the inside. Combined with the salt air it was a delicious lunch.

The sun was so hot and the food was even hotter, yet it was an experience I yearned to re-live many times. I don't ever make fish and chips at home, I save that meal for whenever we go to the beach; it doesn't taste the same without that magical ingredient . . . a sea breeze.

I loved that day at Manly and we went back there often as a family during my early teens. It was the only beach we ever made the effort to go to. We never swam, but we built castles in the sand and watched them wash away. My father was a good swimmer but he was worried the big waves would overwhelm us as the beaches in Australia were open to the sea and so different to the calmer waters we were used to in Saudi Arabia. Nevertheless it was worth the journey, it would take us all day and by the time we got home we were so tired we would smell of the beach and our hands would still smell of fish and chips. On that day it didn't matter, we would head straight to bed exhausted but happy.

As an adult I went back to Manly Beach with my husband nearly twenty years after that first visit and it is still magnificent. It unearthed a love for that place that had been buried for a long time. I sat with Hazem and reminisced at how happy I felt whenever I was there. It is a place that seems oblivious to what is wrong with the world. I wished I was frozen in time in that moment forever.

That long, hot summer holiday my father would take us to many Australian tourist sights: the Opera House, the Chinese Gardens, Darling Harbour and the Blue Mountains, where we tasted the world famous Tasmanian leatherwood honey for the first time. It would become the only honey my parents ever ate in Australia. Honey is one of the earthly pleasures God has mentioned in the Quran alongside a few other things. The Prophet Mohammad taught that it has medicinal qualities like nothing else on earth, internally and externally it has healing qualities and there is not a Muslim home that doesn't have a jar or two in the pantry.

My mother hadn't forgotten how wonderful Annette had been and she kept in touch. She called her and invited her down to see us in Sydney. When Annette arrived she gasped and said 'Look how big they have all gotten!' She hugged and kissed my mother and my mother started to cry. Annette is a special person who had helped my mother enormously when we were living in Grafton. While she was staying with us, my mother and Annette would stand under the jewel tree talking of old times, sharing cups of tea and much, much more. She went back home after a few days and my mother would call her and chat but she never made it to Sydney again because she was busy with her family in Grafton. That was the last time I saw Annette but I know my mother and Annette stayed friends. Despite my judgment of my mother for betraying my secret she taught me how resilient, strong and resourceful women can be. My mother had to learn a new language and raise a family in a new country and she did it well. On this second trip to Australia my father bought our first family car. That Holden Commodore served us well as we only sold it three years ago. It sat there unused whenever my father left on one of his many visits back to Saudi Arabia because my mother didn't have a driver's licence. Just as we had done in Grafton, we'd all troop to the shops with her to carry all the groceries home. It must have taunted her to have a car there but still have to walk everywhere because one day she decided to take some driving lessons and apply for a driver's licence. She didn't tell my father. My mother found a female instructor and every two days she would organise a lesson. For a woman who had never been behind the wheel of a car and was always driven anywhere she wanted to go, that was gutsy.

One day we came home from school to find her waiting for us and smiling like a happy school girl. She showed us her licence. I was so proud of her. It was a bold and brave thing to do, especially without telling anyone. She had regained some of her rights back: her Islamic right to be mobile. For her it was a personal liberation because when she was living in Saudi Arabia women weren't allowed to drive there. Out of respect she didn't drive my father's car. She waited until he returned and then on the night he arrived she told him she now had a licence. He was surprised and didn't really take it well at first, but he got over it because he knew it was her right and before long he was asking her to pick up things for him! My mother showed me that women can do anything if they put their minds to it.

Tatoush salad

Ingredients

2 Lebanese cucumbers
2 large tomatoes
½ a cos lettuce
4 green shallots
5 red radishes
1 cup fresh mint
2 cups chopped Italian parsley
1 cup olive oil (for frying)
½ a Lebanese pita bread

Dressing

2 tbs pomegranate molasses
¼ cup extra virgin olive oil
2 tsp salt
Zest of one lemon

Method

Chop all the vegetables into bite-sized pieces and place into a bowl. Roughly chop the mint and parsley leaves and add to the salad.

In a saucepan heat the olive oil and cut the Lebanese bread into small pieces. Deep-fry them in the oil until golden brown. This should only take a few seconds. Place them onto a paper towel and and when cooled add them to the salad.

In a separate bowl, mix pomegranate molasses with a whisk then add olive oil, salt and lemon zest. Whisk them together. Drizzle over salad, toss and serve.

Serves 4 to 6 people.

Falafel

This is the recipe my mother makes, so it's a mix of Palestinian- and Syrian-style falafel and I think a bit of Egyptian too!

Ingredients

- 1¼ cups dried and peeled fava beans (broad beans) soaked overnight
- 1¼ cup dried chickpeas soaked overnight
- 1 onion
- 3 garlic cloves
- 1 bunch parsley
- 1 bunch coriander
- 2 tbs salt
- 2 tbs flour
- 1 tsp pimento
- 1 tbs ground dried coriander
- ½ tsp chilli powder
- ½ tsp ground black pepper
- 1 tbs ground cumin
- ½ tsp ground cinnamon
- ½ tsp bicarbonate soda
- 1 tbs baking powder
- 500ml of sunflower oil for frying

Method

After soaking the fava beans and chickpeas overnight rinse and drain from the water. Peel and chop onion and garlic into quarters. Wash parsley and coriander well. Grind these ingredients in a meat grinder on the finest setting or use a food processor to grind them into a semi-fine paste. At this stage you can freeze this mixture and defrost when you are ready to use it.

Otherwise add all the other ingredients and mix well. Set aside for an hour for the mixture to rise. Then mix well again and heat the oil. Shape mixture into small balls using a special falafel mould (available from most Middle Eastern grocery stores) or by using your hands. When the falafel is browned on both sides remove from the oil with a slotted spoon and place on a paper towel to drain.

Enjoy with fresh vegies, tahina sauce and pickles.

Makes approximately 70 pieces.

Deep-fried Kibbe

Kibbe filling

Kibbe filling varies from country to country but this is the way my mother makes it.

Ingredients

- 1 tbs butter
- 1 tbs olive oil
- 1 large onion, chopped finely
- 500g medium ground lean lamb mince
- 2 tsp ground cumin
- 1 tsp pimento
- 1 tsp cinnamon
- ½ tsp hot paprika
- 1 tbs salt
- 1 tsp ground black pepper
- 1 tbs pomegranate molasses
- 1 cup roughly chopped walnuts or ½ cup of toasted pine nuts

Ingredients for kibbe dough

- 2 medium onions
- 500g fine brown burghul, washed and drained well
- 500g kibbe mince from your local Halal butcher
- 1 tsp salt
- 1 tbs ground cumin
- ½ tsp black pepper
- ½ tsp cinnamon

½ tsp pimento
½ tsp hot paprika

Method for kibbe filling
In a large frypan melt the butter and oil. Add the onion and sauté until translucent. Add the mince and sauté until juices have dried out. Add all the dried spices and mix. Take the mixture off the heat and add the pomegranate molasses and walnuts (or browned pine nuts in some butter) and mix well.

Method for kibbe dough
In a food processor chop the onions very finely, adding the washed and drained burghul to the mix. Place over the kibbe mince in a bowl. Add all the spices and mix with your hands. Wet your hands with some water to avoid it sticking.

Method for filling kibbe
To make deep-fried kibbe take a portion of the kibbe dough and roll it into a ball in your palm. With your pointer finger begin to push a hole in the middle of the ball while turning it, widening the hole as you create a shell for the filling. Once the edges have thinned insert a spoon of the kibbe filling and gather the dough edges and seal it. Continue to shape it into a small lemon shape and place on to a tray ready for frying. Heat up the oil in a deep saucepan, (I like to use half olive oil and half sunflower oil) and watch them brown. Remove from the oil and place on paper towels to drain then serve hot.

Makes approximately 20 individual kibbe. Serves 10 people.

Palestinian Mansaf Asmaa-style (rice with lamb and cooked yoghurt)

Ingredients for cooking the lamb (bone stock)

- 1kg lamb neck trimmed and cut into 2cm wide pieces
- 1kg trimmed lamb shoulder cut into large pieces
- 2 tsp salt
- 1 tsp ground black pepper
- 1 tsp ground pimento
- 1 tsp ground cinnamon
- 1 tsp turmeric
- 2 bay leaves
- 1 large onion, quartered

Ingredients for the yoghurt

- 2kg Greek-style set yoghurt
- 3 tbs cornflour dissolved in some cold water
- 3 cups bone stock (prepared earlier)
- 2 tsp salt
- ½ tsp turmeric

Ingredients for the rice

- 4 cups long-grain rice, soaked for 20 minutes, and drained
- 6 cups bone stock (prepared earlier)
- 1 cup slivered almonds
- 1 tbs butter

Some pine nuts
2 tsp salt
½ tsp turmeric

Method

Place the lamb neck and shoulder in a pot of boiling water, boil the meat for 15 minutes then discard the water and start again in a clean pressure cooker (this removes all the impurities from the stock which is the basis for cooking the rice and yoghurt). After refreshing the water add all the spices, bay leaves and quartered onion and bring to the boil. Cook for 35 minutes and set aside. Meanwhile place the yoghurt in a large pot and add dissolved cornflour and mix. When pressure cooker is ready to open render the fat then add the strained stock to the yoghurt and mix well. Add salt and turmeric.

Soak the rice for 20 minutes. Place drained rice in a separate pot and add strained stock to cover the rice by 2cm (use the spoon method in 'Kabsa with chicken' to check stock level). Bring to the boil and simmer on low heat.

Place the yoghurt on medium heat and stir continuously until it comes to the boil, otherwise it will curdle. This should take about 15 minutes. Reduce the heat and begin to slowly place the strained meat and bones into the cooked yoghurt, simmer for 5 minutes. Remove the meat and set aside. In a frypan place the butter and almonds and begin to brown them. Halfway through add the pine nuts. Toss until they are golden brown.

When the rice is ready place it in a large communal serving dish and top with strained meat. Sprinkle with browned almonds and pine nuts.

In some parts of Palestine a few layers of traditional bread called *marquq* are added (commonly known in the West as lavash bread). This thin wholemeal paper-like bread is popular in Palestine. It is placed beneath the bed of rice which makes it soft so it tears away when you cut it. Run the hot cooked yoghurt through a sieve and serve it in a large bowl.

To eat this amazing soul food place a portion of rice and meat in a bowl and pour some hot yoghurt over it. Wait a few minutes for the rice to absorb some of the yoghurt and then enjoy.

Serves from 6 to 8 people.

Chapter Five

A Different World

At the beginning of 1990, after that wonderful Christmas holiday was over, Maha, Reem and I started at high school. While Firas was going to Liverpool West Public our parents had enrolled us at Liverpool Girls' High. My mother had her hands full looking after Mohammad.

It was a confusing time for me. According to my faith I would be wearing the veil if we were still in Saudi Arabia, but my parents were not asking us to do so in Australia. I am sure they were concerned about us fitting in. We were only supposed to be there for a year and Liverpool had only a small population of Muslims at the time so you didn't see many veiled women around. In my parents' eyes it was easier to blend in if we dressed the same as everyone else. They were unsure how people would react to us wearing a veil. My mother did not wear her veil when we first arrived. I always knew that she lost a lot of herself when she made that difficult decision to take off her veil out of fear of being outcast. My mother found herself again and decided to wear it in 1995 when she was going to be interviewed for the teacher's job in TAFE. She walked into the interview wearing her veil proudly and walked out with a job that lasted over seventeen years. The recent decisions by governments like France to take away the basic human right of any woman to wear the hijab in government schools, universities and work places is a step backwards in the rights of women. Any woman should have the basic right to dress in the manner she feels comfortable.

As I entered high school I wasn't just dealing with life in a new country, I had to deal with forgoing all that was familiar to me. I was someone who thought about things a great deal; I questioned everything in my mind. I had strong opinions but I kept them, mostly, to myself.

My sisters and I had to catch the bus to school and we would walk through a small park at the end of our street to reach the bus stop. This park overlooked a small rainwater creek and on its banks, growing wild, were the biggest dill bushes I had ever seen. Dill is a very hardy herb, much hardier than it looks with its wispy fern-like appearance. I showed them to my grandmother, who was visiting and she picked some stalks to chew on. As she bit in the juice filled her mouth and I could see it was a sensation she enjoyed. After that she would ask me to pick her a few stalks on my way home from school every day. Finally my mother and I walked over to the creek one weekend and dug out one of the small bushes and transplanted it in our front garden so Hindiya could come out of the house whenever she felt like it and pick some of the long stalks and feathery leaves.

Middle Eastern cooking uses dill fresh and dry and it is one of the spices that features in the Moroccan couscous my mother makes. It is delicious. She seals the lamb pieces then cooks it in a stock of onions with dry dill seeds, bay leaves, cinnamon and black pepper. In another pot she sautés chopped onions and pumpkins and when they change in colour she adds tomatoes, chicken stock, more dill seeds and a cup or two of chickpeas then cooks it all till tender. The lamb is added to the vegetables and then laid on a bed of couscous and drizzled with the stock. Whenever she makes it the whole house is perfumed with the smell of the aromatic herbs and my mouth starts watering as soon as I smell it cooking.

The best part of the school day was the walk back home through that park. And possibly the worst was the actual bus ride. Those first few weeks were particularly daunting as we didn't know anyone and the bus was full of girls and boys, teenage boys especially, who looked very questioningly at the three new sisters who never spoke to anyone.

There was one particular Australian boy who was two years older who took a curious liking to me. He tried to talk to me many times but my older sister Maha disapproved. He was very polite and seemed fascinated with our eyes. 'You all have such beautiful eyes, with gorgeous long eyelashes,' he would say. Every morning he would smile and say 'hello' and every morning we would all ignore him until one day I turned around and said 'hello' in return. Maha frowned at me but I was only trying to be polite. And the truth was I was also curious; what could be so bad about talking with boys? I had never had a friendship with a boy I wasn't related to before. And this one seemed lovely, he was much kinder than some of the girls on that bus. I was just responding to a friendly face.

School was difficult. I felt stupid most of the time. When it came to English I felt as though I was dyslexic. I was confused as to which vowel did what where. I learned how to avoid reading out loud in class. I would raise my hand and ask to be excused to go to the bathroom or I'd change my seat so it wouldn't be my turn. It was all so exhausting, trying to stay under the teacher's radar. Homework would take twice as long as it should have because

I would use the dictionary for every second word. I couldn't ask Maha and Reem to help me because they had their own problems adjusting and keeping up with their own work.

Dad would help with maths and science as, thankfully, the languages of numbers and creation were universal. I was doing maths in Year Seven that I had learned in Year Five in Saudi Arabia. The level of education was different to that in Saudi Arabia, so it meant I was ahead in some areas. But it still pained me to struggle so much with English and feel so disconnected from everyone else. And I wasn't the only one.

There might not have been a big Muslim community in Liverpool but there were a lot of different ethnic groups. There were children from South America, Asia, India, Europe, the Mediterranean and many Pacific Islands, to name a few. I am sure they all had to deal with similar issues as we did.

Despite the troubles I felt adjusting to this new life, I came to see this as one of the great privileges of my life in Australia. We can walk down the street and there is the chance of meeting someone from nearly every country. Even as a teenager I knew this was a gift. The way Australia can become home while still allowing a person the freedom to carry with them the traditions of a former homeland – what a delightful and enriching experience that is. It makes me feel privileged to be among people of different backgrounds and learn about them without leaving home. I love that an entire suburb can be dubbed Little Italy or Chinatown for its high density of people who all come from that country and bring with them the food and customs to share.

I love walking somewhere like Norton Street in Leichhardt in Sydney, eating the food and buying produce and products. I always go there for Italian olive tapenade made from the fruits of the trees in Italy; the rich earth in Italy makes the olives taste so unique. I also buy sundried tomatoes and occasionally jars of pesto that are a part of many of the Italian recipes we make at home. I make my own pesto most of the time, lots of fresh basil and parmesan cheese with garlic and walnuts instead of pine nuts. Some lemon juice and zest, a dash of salt and a heap of extra virgin olive oil. Fresh and green mixed with freshly boiled spaghetti, a simple toss and it's ready to eat.

By this, our second stay in Sydney, we noticed things starting to change in Liverpool. In the early nineties there were more migrants from different countries and even an Arabic grocer who sold products from all over the Middle East. We had a place where we could buy orange blossom water and tahina; pomegranate molasses and Arabic bread and *za'atar,* the oregano mix every Arab loves. Liverpool had its own Lebanese sweet shop with a fresh bakery that made all the different *Manoush,* the traditional Arab pizza that was topped with cheese and mince, spinach and *za'atar,* that was breakfast for the family on Mum's day off.

It made life a whole lot easier for my mother when she didn't have to travel for half an hour to pick up some of the everyday groceries that were part of the traditional Middle Eastern dishes she cooked. By then, Liverpool even had its own Halal butcher, who kept all the cuts of meat for cooking traditional Arabic dishes. In Saudi Arabia there is only Halal meat but in Grafton it wasn't available so we did without it for the whole time we lived there. My mother would use as a substitute for meat all the different fish and seafood that was available. It is very different today as Halal food is available in most places. The term 'Halal' is one that many people are confused by, but there is no mystery about it. It quite simply means 'permissible under Islamic law'. This law lays out a very technical process that outlines how an animal is slaughtered. Under Islamic guidelines the animal must be killed with a clean cut to the throat and in one motion severing the main arteries allowing the blood to drain from the carcass, while blessing it by saying 'in the name of Allah'. The blood is then left to drain from the carcass. Modern Western society is beginning to understand its benefits, although Muslims have been practising this for over 1400 years. The meat is healthier and keeps better and longer. But the term Halal is also used to describe foods that are *permitted* to be eaten; these are foods not containing alcohol or any products from pigs, whether it be meat or fat or by-products.

As with other religions, not everything in Islam has an immediate explanation. Some issues were unfamiliar to Prophet Mohammad as some things were before his time, and others only became relevant to Muslims as time and humanity evolved. The prophet would explain that these issues are for future generations to learn from and will be revealed in due time. In the understanding of Muslims some aspects of science are yet to catch up to the Quran's teachings.

The way the Liverpool community began to adapt to its growing ethnic population helped us feel more at home, but none of us ever felt very stable as my parents were still set on returning to Saudi Arabia in the near future. It might sound strange that they wanted to give their children a country of their own and yet they weren't going to live there constantly. But this plan made sense for them financially and the isolation my mother felt with her limited English must have contributed to their decision. Thank goodness she had my uncle nearby.

My father was travelling back to Saudi Arabia every three months to make sure he kept his working visa as he was not confident of finding consistent employment or a stable income in Australia. With five children and a wife to support this was critical. In the early days he'd fly over to Saudi Arabia to make sure his visa was stamped and he'd make sure our home was still okay, stay a few weeks and then fly back. It was a costly exercise but a necessary one as he was struggling to find consistent work in Australia. But, as it became obvious that my father would have difficulty finding work as an engineer in Australia, he spent longer and longer periods in Saudi Arabia. My mother was left in Australia to cope on her own.

Meanwhile, I knew this time in Australia was going to be brief, so it was hard for me to find a sense of place. It was the same as when we'd gone back to Saudi Arabia after our time in Grafton; I never felt settled or completely part of either country. Every time we moved my sense of belonging moved with me. We didn't know it but all that was about to change.

Our first Ramadan in Liverpool was in March of 1990. We hadn't been back at school long and I was still trying to make my way. During Ramadan we fast from sunrise to sunset. Summer daylight savings hours were in place so we were fasting for nearly fourteen hours. It meant we couldn't eat until after eight in the evening. With the Islamic calendar rotation it would be the Middle East's turn to fast during summer hours in a few years time so no part of the world had an unfair advantage because of the hemisphere they were in. Another example of Islam's equality for all.

Ramadan is the holiest month of the Islamic calendar as it is the month when the message of Islam was bestowed upon Prophet Mohammad by the angel Gabriel. It is a month of sacrifice and I have been taught it is important to feel the hunger and pain of people less fortunate than I. It's a month of caring for your body and cleansing it by giving your digestive system a rest for a few hours a day. It is also a month of giving *zakat* (charity). It is about discipline and self-control. It is a month of patience and prayer, a month of forgiveness and giving. Ramadan is followed by the first of two *Eid* festivities in the Islamic calendar. The *Eid* after Ramadan is called *Eid-al-Fitr*, meaning the end of fast. Muslims all around the world celebrate this *Eid* at the same time but in different ways. Islam is not a culture, it is a religion, so it doesn't enforce the Arabian way just because the Quran is in Arabic. Cultural diversity is respected in Islam and encouraged as long as it doesn't clash with religious rules. For example, Muslims in Indonesia and Malaysia practise Islam the same way Muslims in Turkey and Saudi Arabia do but the cultural differences are still visible and apparent, which keeps diversity wonderfully preserved. The foods of each country are also different during Ramadan and *Eid*, people in the Middle East make *mamoul* filled with dates for *Eid*, while Malaysians make their famous jelly desserts in all colours and flavours.

I'd always loved Ramadan because one of the things that makes it special is getting together with family and friends. That year was different. It made me more aware of my family's differences and I felt very lonely. Even though there had been an increase in Middle Eastern migration to the Liverpool area there were no mosques nearby. The only one we knew of was in Lakemba in Sydney's west, which was too far to travel to. There were no calls to prayer, no nights lit with Ramadan lanterns and no big family dinners with every food you craved in sight. We all felt the same and missed Saudi Arabia very much at this time.

Instead of the huge extended family gatherings we were used to, we had only my uncle and his family to share Ramadan with and it was not the same. My mother did as she always did and picked the vine leaves in the backyard to make a dish my uncle hadn't tasted in years. It's called *warak enab*, which is rolled vine leaves with a mix of rice and mince on the inside. She would put in a few stuffed zucchinis and some lamb neck and then lay them down carefully in a deep pot one by one and they would all cook in the bone stock. This dish and many variations of it, including a vegetarian version, are made across the Middle East and the Mediterranean and in some places it's referred to as *dolma* or *dolmades*. There are so many variations and some are served hot and others cold. My research suggests that they came from Turkey originally. Turkish cuisine is responsible for many dishes popular around the world, including shish kebab, babaganoush and baklava to name a few. Geographically linking Arabia, Asia and Europe in the passage of trade on the silk route to Europe, Turkey had developed its cuisine through adapting many different spices, cooking techniques, produce and flavours over the centuries. In Ottoman times, Istanbul was a cosmopolitan blend of different nationalities each bringing their own cuisine. This is the reason Turkish cuisine has a rich blend.

It would take my mother all day to finish filling the vine leaves but when my sisters and I got home from school we would lend a hand. I would try and mark the ones I rolled so I could eat them myself. My mother would lay them out on a huge tray, they were like little fingers topped with fresh lemon juice. The smell of cooked vine leaves is a strong one and unique. After they were cooked I could never tell which were mine but it didn't matter because they all tasted so delicious.

The celebrations during Ramadan meant we ate foods that we didn't eat all year round. Just like Christmas pudding for Anglo-Australians; we could eat these foods at other times if we wanted to but it just tastes that much better when it is saved for a celebration. And the dishes tasted even better because we were fasting. The sweet dish *katayef* is my most beloved Ramadan sweet. These are small pancakes stuffed with *ashta*, the Arab cream.

They can be filled with chopped walnuts with a mix of sugar, cinnamon and nutmeg. The pancakes are toasted and dipped in a sugar syrup; they are traditionally deep fried in oil but are a lot healthier toasted. With one bite the crunchy nuts melt into your mouth. A sweet cheese can also be put into the filling and it melts when you toast it. I love all the variations and 'just heavenly' is the only way I can describe it.

During that Ramadan we tried our best not to miss home so much. It helped that my grandmother was with us. We would gather around and listen to her and my mother talk about how important Ramadan is and all the good deeds we were getting for fasting for such long hours. My grandmother would keep us fascinated with stories of Prophet Mohammad and his *hadith*, all the sayings and stories of his life. I would hear Mum softly reciting the Quran late at night. Her voice would reach my room and I would feel safe and peaceful.

But not everyone was at peace. Across the other side of the world events were occurring that would impact on our lives in a way we could never predict. In Australia, we were far removed from international politics and the threat of war; however, in August 1990 international events would predetermine the rest of our lives. The first Gulf War began and my parents were glued to the television almost twenty-four hours a day watching the news reports in disbelief. We were only supposed to be in Australia for a year to finish our residency and earn the right to our precious citizenship and a chance to call a country ours. For all of us, up to that point Saudi Arabia was still the place we thought of as home. The Gulf War changed everything.

War affected our lives in a dramatic way even though we were never under fire or ducking under bombs. We were indirect refugees. This is one of the hidden effects of war on people and societies –

being displaced or uprooted from your home without being under any physical harm can be devastating. In many cases families lose everything – their home, their proximity to family, the chance to work in the profession they are educated for, their sense of safety. All this can happen without actually being in the war zone.

Most of the Arab world was shocked at the international community's willingness to get involved when there had been so many other conflicts around the world that were just as deserving of swift action. Places like Palestine and Israel, for example. But the Arabs were no fools, oil was the motivating factor for the US-led coalition, not human rights violations. The fact that Saddam Hussein had been their ally in the Middle East and they'd supplied him with all the artillery he needed when he was at war with Iran meant they knew what he was capable of. They wanted to step in quickly and were ready to strike.

We were in limbo waiting for the war to be over. My father worried terribly and made numerous phone calls to his family in Saudi Arabia to make sure they were safe, and to his boss to see if there was still a job available for him. No one knew what was going to happen. All people could do was sit and wait.

During that uncertain time my parents received a letter from the Department of Immigration informing us that we had completed our residency requirements and could apply for our citizenship. Because of what was happening in the Middle East the whole thing took on an ever greater poignancy. Without a working visa my father and mother had no country to call home either. I look back now and can't even imagine what that felt like for them. It must have been distressing to be displaced a second time, to have a family depending on them and not knowing if they could make a living.

That letter was a gift from the heavens but it also signalled the end of all that they knew. In October 1990 my family walked over to Liverpool Council Chambers and my parents, Maha and Reem took the oath with a hundred or so other families. Firas, Mohammad and I stayed home, as Mum thought we might get restless if it were a long ceremony. Just like that we became Australians. My parents were so thankful for that piece of paper. It was our safety net, and they had achieved what they set out to do, they had enabled *all* their children to have a country to call home.

Despite my parents' delight, and despite having certificates of citizenship, my sense of belonging in Australia had not increased. I was still a person of two worlds and unsure of where I should be. School was nearly over for that year and my parents had many conversations about our chances of returning to Saudi Arabia. With no employment on the horizon in Australia, Dad decided he would have to go back on his own to see if things were okay for us to return. Things weren't good in Saudi Arabia and my father was frustrated when he lost his job. Fortunately his former boss promised he would organise a working visa for him even though there was no work and in this way ensure he could at least travel over to see his family.

With things in the Middle East looking grim, my parents now saw all our futures in Australia. Dad was focused on finding work, so early every Saturday morning I would go with him on what would become a weekly ritual for the next fifteen years. We would go to the local newsagency to buy *The Sydney Morning Herald*, which had the biggest classifieds section. We'd then walk back home and I'd make him a pot of traditional Turkish coffee with the coffee he'd brought back with him from Saudi Arabia. The coffee was ground with cardamom and the aroma would fill the house. Dad would sit looking through the paper, highlighting the jobs he'd apply for. He had multiple copies of his résumé ready to send out. I would often join him in a cup of coffee. I loved it, just me and Dad sharing a quiet morning. This coffee has become a family favourite and over the years every time Dad went to Saudi Arabia he'd bring back a few kilos. Brewed with precision, we enjoyed it bitter with soft sweet dates to eat on the side. Even now, as an adult, I still drink that coffee and I had a box shipped over to Sydney a few years ago when Dad's supply ran out.

I remember being in the study with Dad years later, when he was clearing out some old paperwork. He took out a box and showed me the hundred or so rejection letters he'd received over the years. Dad explained how some companies he applied to would like him on paper but when he was given the opportunity for an interview they would meet him and never call him back. He never knew whether it was his accent or his appearance. He had a mountain of experience in projects far more complex than what he was applying for but so many weren't prepared to give him a go.

The reason they gave was always the same: 'You're over-qualified for the job', is what they would say. How ridiculous. If you can have someone working for you who can do the job, and you can also benefit from their experience in other areas, why wouldn't you give them a job? I had no idea this was happening at the time and it must have been tough for him to stay optimistic. He did everything by the book; he became a member of Engineers Australia to stay informed about the industry, made hundreds of phone calls, he was always clean-shaven and well-dressed in a suit, and was willing to do anything. But the reality was his degree and his many years of experience in Saudi Arabia, working on enormous projects as the head project manager with American companies, meant nothing. After so many knockbacks my father became convinced that engineering in Australia was a closed-shop boys' club and he had no hope of being part of it. It meant he was forced to keep travelling overseas to earn an income to support his family.

My father is a proud man and like so many men he sees it as his duty to provide. I know it pained him leaving us all to fend without him every time he went away. He was concerned with earning money to feed, clothe and house us all. But it would bring him some comfort that Mum had three brothers in Sydney at that time because by then Uncle Moaz and Uncle Bara'a had also moved to Australia.

From the hundreds of applications he submitted only two jobs came about, one of those jobs lasted just three months and the other came through a referral from an old workmate in Saudi Arabia who put in a good word for Dad. The job was with an Italian engineer who was working alongside his two engineer sons. This man appreciated my dad's experience and hired him to work on the refurbishment of Central Station in the heart of Sydney.

It is such a terrible feeling for a man, and especially a father, not to be able to provide for his family the way he has for years. I knew my father felt frustrated and useless and he would be unapproachable at times and obviously stressed. We were spending our savings and the lack of opportunity was depressing for him. His inability to find work and his resulting frustration took a toll on his relationship with my mother. He was a proud, educated man who had always provided for his family and now, in a new country, he was out of his depth.

My mother was also finding her way but she was pushing boundaries, like getting her driver's licence, and he realised how different things were. I was excited for him when he finally found this job and he was getting up early and heading off to work just like old times. But the lack of full-time work and the threat of unemployment always hovered over him as he did not feel respected and appreciated in his profession in Australia. He worked overseas irregularly and at other times he would go to Saudi Arabia just to see his family. His time away kept getting longer and longer. Personally, I feel the engineering industry could have really benefitted from my father's expertise.

My grandmother Hindiya had the same feelings of displacement about Australia. She loved to visit often but when Uncle Mohammad and my mother ever asked her to consider staying in Australia permanently she would refuse. I would hear her say how she thought Australia was a beautiful country, organised and developed, but here she felt insignificant. People didn't know who she was, and sometimes she was looked at in a way she didn't appreciate. She didn't speak English and didn't move quickly and if she was in someone's way, say on the escalator at the shopping centre, she would hear people speak to her with a frustrated tone that didn't sound kind at all.

She would say that no matter how bad things were economically in Syria, she was still able to walk down her street and everyone there would know who she was and greet her, offering her a cup of coffee and help if she was carrying groceries. She knew she would miss the call to prayer and the month of Ramadan that was seen and felt everywhere. Hindiya had her roots there and a family history she wasn't willing to forfeit for the second time, for a few comforts she had learned to live without. This is echoed in many stories of people who leave their homeland for better opportunities in foreign lands. The reception is not always with open arms and it takes years for people to re-establish themselves in a new home and build a sense of community while preserving and passing on their heritage for the new generations of their family. Many can do it once but to have to try again is too hard. That is how my grandmother felt.

I knew that my dad had his struggles and that the Gulf War was partly to blame, but I didn't know that the Saudi Arabian government unofficially withdrew many working visas for migrants who were from countries that had criticised the war in Iraq and the position the Saudi Arabian government was taking. This meant many people who had lived in Saudi Arabia for years, people whose families had grown up there, were sent back to their country. Generations of families were suddenly uprooted and had to leave all that was familiar. What would have been the logic behind all this? How were these people at fault? I am glad I didn't know about all this at the time as it was hard enough trying to deal with what I *was* aware of. The changes that were happening and the way, suddenly, a life can change is difficult for anyone to deal with. Experiences like this humble you as a human being, but all I wanted as a teenager at the time was to feel like I belonged.

At high school there were twenty or so Arabic-speaking girls from Year Seven to Year Twelve. They were from many different countries in the Middle East. It took me a whole year to get to know some of them and, once I did, I would join them at lunchtime. We'd sit together and take out our Arabic bread rolls filled with thick *Labneh,* a thickened yoghurt that was drizzled with olive oil, and olives. These girls reminded me of my friends overseas and I was looking for what was familiar. But after a few months I realised that the only things we had in common were that we spoke the same language and ate the same food.

It wasn't widespread but the Gulf War did increase the hostility being directed at Liverpool's small Arab Muslim residents by the ignorant few. I remember a friend telling me years later of an incident that could have easily made a person bitter and hateful. The week Australia announced its deployment of troops to the Middle East to join in the war, my friend, her sister and her brother were being walked to school by their mother when they were attacked in the main street of Miller, a suburb of Liverpool. Two men chased them with sticks and tree branches they picked up off the footpath. They hit her mother across the back while one tried to rip her veil off her head. Bystanders did nothing as her mother sheltered them and, as they cried, she told them not to be scared. No matter what her mother said she couldn't shield her daughter's eyes from what was going on. But remarkably this friend never hated or directed her feelings from that incident at other Australians; her mother taught her that those men were an exception and that not everyone was like them. This friend and her family were Lebanese and she was born in Australia and her country had nothing to do with the Gulf War. They learned not to hate or fear the community they lived in, but other children of migrants were not so inclined because they too were on the receiving end of the small minority who didn't hide their feelings about not wanting 'strangers' in their country.

Some of the girls I befriended were frustrated and angry with the way they weren't fitting in easily and they would show this to the teachers and to the Australian students. They would find any reason to have a fight with the Australians at lunchtime. Some of the Australian girls didn't hold back either, they would provoke them by calling them 'Wog' and 'Filthy Arab' away from the ears of teachers. I was horrified by both sides. What appeared to be unfounded anger from the children of migrants was actually their way of preserving their sense of self in the country in which they were born but from a society where they felt excluded. And the Australian girls were experiencing something similar, trying to stick to and protect what they knew and were more comfortable with. That prejudice would even find its way towards some of the newer teachers at school with hints of accents in their speech. They were made fun of by both migrant and Australian teens for sounding and looking different.

It took me a year or two to work out I that I didn't want to hang out with these girls. I had needed to find a place I belonged and had grabbed hold of these girls just because they had the same heritage. But they didn't see things the way I did, so I decided they were not the company I should keep. I wanted to find my way in my new country, but not with anger and by separating myself from new possibilities. This initial eagerness to make the wrong friends would affect my relationships with my sisters, who didn't understand why I felt like I had to fit in so desperately. My growing friendship with the boy on the bus and my association with these girls caused my sisters and my mother to think I was slipping away. At this stage I was fifteen or sixteen.

As the weeks rolled by, the boy on the bus, Clayton, and I would chat every morning, with both Maha and Reem disapproving greatly and watching us very closely. Clayton was tall with blond curly hair and freckles. He spoke softly and was quite popular. He wanted to know all about me and where I was from. Of course I responded to him. He wasn't looking down on me, he was treating me with friendship and respect. He was fascinated by our foreignness and he would go off and research Saudi Arabia and the next day he would ask new questions. After a year of chatting on the bus, he started to tell me how much he liked me. On Valentine's Day 1991 he got off the bus at the shops in Liverpool and walked the rest of the way to school. All my friends ran up to me in the playground shouting all sorts of things. I couldn't understand what they were saying but they dragged me to the common area we shared with the boys' school next door and there was Clayton with twelve long-stemmed red roses, waiting for me.

One of my friends pushed me towards him. I was so embarrassed. Clayton looked at me and said, 'These are for you; happy Valentine's Day.' I took the roses quite nervously, all red-faced and frightened, wondering how I was going to explain them to my parents! It was a flattering and grand gesture for a Year Eight girl to get such beautiful and expensive roses but I didn't know what Clayton wanted in return. He looked disappointed when he walked away. I know now he was probably expecting a kiss as a thank you. From that day on I was called 'the girl who got the roses' by the students *and* the teachers.

Year Eight was an eye-opener in a lot of ways for me. It was when they started sex education in school. My mother signed the permission note without giving me any warning of what I was about to learn. I was horrified when details about sex were outlined. I couldn't even imagine what the teacher was explaining. My parents had preserved our innocence as much as they could. If two people were even kissing during the TV show *Neighbours* my parents would change the channel as we would all shy away and turn our heads. I still do that with my own kids these days.

I was overwhelmed by this new knowledge of sex and suddenly felt so disrespected to be pursued by boys for those reasons – why can't we just talk! It seemed suddenly to colour everything. Why can't we enjoy each other's company without all that trouble? From then on it seemed any interaction between a male and female revolved around sex and that was something I didn't like. If a girl was kind or nice she was a flirt, and if she was respectful she was being 'stuck up and bitchy or frigid'. The boys chased and it seemed that mostly the girls enjoyed being chased, but there were moments in which the girls did the chasing too. Why hadn't I noticed any of this before? It would take me a few more years to realise how this really affected me, and how I saw women perceived in society. It is something I would forever be trying to understand. I would be pursued by boys many times over the years and I grew more resentful because they all eventually wanted more than my friendship.

Towards the end of Year Ten I finally disconnected completely from the group of friends I'd made in Year Seven and I met my first veiled friend in Australia, Abeer. She was new to the school, but had arrived in Australia four years before, like me. Her father was Palestinian and her mother was Lebanese and she was born in Kuwait and was living there when the Gulf War began. Her family fled and, like us, with no country to unite them Australia was the answer. Australia took in a small number of refugees from Kuwait during the war. My future brother-in-law, Akheel, who married my sister Reem, would be from one of those families who found a new home in Australia. Akheel and his family were Palestinians and he was born in Kuwait. He was another second-generation Palestinian who had never seen Palestine because of the Israeli occupation.

Abeer and I connected instantly and we remain friends today. I remember walking through the local shopping centre with her and feeling so angry at the way some people would look at her because she was wearing the veil. I would turn to her and say, 'Doesn't that bother you, how many dirty looks you're getting?' And she would say, 'You get used to it after a while.' That would make me even angrier.

The strangers who saw only her veil judged her by her appearance. I was a teenager, a Muslim and into the same things as Abeer, but because I looked like everybody else I was not judged

A Different World

the same way. I know we all do this every day – judge someone on their appearance and form opinions about a person's character because of their clothing – but my friendship with Abeer meant I tried to fight against doing this whenever I would catch myself.

The many experiences with Abeer deterred me from ever considering the veil during my teenage years. I dressed conservatively and was offended by the unwanted and often objectionable sexual attention boys would give me. But I was too scared of being judged and being typecast as someone who wasn't Australian enough to dress like other Australians. Most people thought I was Italian or Greek, not Arab or Palestinian, so I wasn't a mystery; but I would witness prejudice against my Arab friends many times and it bothered me a great deal.

Most people's knowledge of Islam and the Middle East in Australia was minimal at that time. In my experience they had never heard of some of the countries in the region, all they knew was that hummus and tabouli were great to eat. At school a teacher once asked me where I was from and when I told her I was Palestinian, she said 'Pakistani?' in amazement. I had to show the teacher my country on a map and point to it. How could it be that the place in which all three holy religions are linked was unknown to some of the Christian people I met here in Australia? This baffled me. I was sure they sang of Bethlehem in Christmas songs. I couldn't understand: what was the missing link?

I was truly surprised that so few knew about the place my family came from and I felt so insignificant at times. I would do my best to learn about Australian history and culture through school and I would have loved to have been taught more about the Middle East and Islam but it wasn't part of the school curriculum. Some of the English novels we read that were about migrant stories, like *Looking for Alibrandi* by Melina Marchetta, were of other cultures finding their way in Australia but we read none about my culture. When I read *My Place* by Sally Morgan I empathised with the Aborigines in Australia and what they had experienced. I felt sad many times as I learned the things that had happened to the Aboriginal people as a result of British settlement, of how indigenous people lost their identity, traditions and culture. I gave a class speech about their experiences and felt a huge sense of injustice for their stolen generations. I applauded when the National Sorry Day officially recognised the tragedy of what had happened to the stolen generations. Perhaps I identified with them because I felt displaced too.

I have since learned about the Muslim cameleers, who came to Australia in the mid to late 1800s and were so important in the development of outback Australia. Not many Australians know of these Afghans and their history. They are called Australia's first Muslim pioneers of the outback. What a magnificent role to have in the discovery of outback Australia. They had built the foundations of the telegraph and railway tracks into the outback. The train line that runs tours across the outback nowadays is named The Ghan in honour of these cameleers. If only history classes had included stories of them and how these Muslim immigrants wove into the fabric of Australia and played a part in building the new nation, it would have helped me feel more of a connection and a sense of belonging sooner. It might have reduced prejudice against Muslim migrants and maybe could have made a difference for the troublesome girls.

Reading about others who had a sense of loss opened my eyes to a lot of injustice and cruelty in the world. It made me realise I was not alone in my struggle to belong and that there were many people trying to make a place for themselves. I kept trying to educate myself and began to read books by female authors, and stories about Aborigines in Australia and African slavery in America. In economics I did a case study about Sierra Leone and the underdeveloped nations and their struggle with imperialism. I was devastated to learn what man had done to others in the name of civilisation and to gain power all over the world. Growing up with such strong women around me, women who had put aside everything for their husbands and children, gave me a strong sense of female pride and these women, my grandmother and mother, fostered in me a questioning nature.

So many of us are shocked at the way greed and control can drive a human being to kill another human being. I suddenly opened my eyes to the sometimes harsh realities of the world and I wanted to do something. I became a teenager on a mission to find out the truth about everything I wondered about. I formed strong opinions and many of them I still carry with me today, some have softened as I get older, others have sharpened. I wanted to live in a world where civilisation improved and advanced an already existing culture or society, preserving what was good about the old and enhancing it with the new, not getting rid of it. I still want that.

In my mind there is too much focus on difference and not enough on our shared humanity. So much bad will and anger comes from fear of the unknown, be it religion, dress or skin colour that suggest difference. It all goes back to us sitting around the table and sharing a meal together. Our basic needs are the same, so why is there so much conflict? I guess that is the age-old question and better minds than mine have failed to answer it. All I can do is treat people how I would like them to treat me and my family. William Shakespeare had the right idea: 'Love all . . . do wrong to none.'

Moroccan couscous (with pumpkins)

Ingredients for cooking meat
- 1 onion, chopped
- 2 tbs vegetable oil
- 1kg lamb in large pieces
- 2 tsp salt
- ½ tsp ground black pepper
- ½ tsp ground cinnamon
- ½ tsp ground pimento
- 2 tbs ground dill seed
- 2 bay leaves
- 1.5 litres hot water

Ingredients for cooking vegetables
- 2 tbs vegetable oil
- 500g onions, chopped into large pieces (approximately 4)
- 1kg pumpkins, chopped into large pieces
- 500g tomatoes, cut into quarters
- 1 litre chicken stock
- 2 tsp salt
- ½ tsp ground black pepper
- ½ tsp ground cinnamon
- ½ tsp ground pimento
- ½ tsp dried chilli flakes
- 2 tbs ground dill seed
- 1 × 400g can chickpeas

Ingredients for couscous
   1 × 500g box of couscous
   chicken stock
   dill seeds
   parsley, chopped

Method for cooking meat
In a pressure cooker sauté one finely chopped onion and 2 tbs of oil for 5 minutes then add the meat and seal. Add all the spices and bay leaves and cook for 5 minutes. Top with hot water and cook for 35 minutes or till tender. Discard the stock.

Method for cooking vegetables
In a large pot heat the oil and sauté onions for 10 minutes. Then add pumpkins and sauté for another 5 minutes. Place tomatoes on top, add the stock and cover. Cook for 20 minutes or until tender. Add the spices, chickpeas and cooked meat pieces to the vegetables and cook for a further 10 minutes. Remove the meat and vegetables from the stock and place on a bed of couscous. Serve the stock and extra vegetables in a separate bowl to be drizzled on each individual plate when served.

(Follow the cooking instructions on the box of couscous using chicken stock instead of water. When ready toss with a few dill seeds and chopped parsley.)

Serves 6 to 8 people.

Katayef

Ingredients
- 1 bag of katayef (pancakes) – approximately 18 pieces – found at most Middle Eastern grocers or sweet shops
- 1½ cups walnuts
- 1½ tsp ground cinnamon
- 1 tbs sugar
- ¼ tsp ground nutmeg
- 2 tbs melted butter

Sugar syrup
- 1 cup sugar
- ½ cup water
- ½ tsp lemon juice
- 1 tbs orange blossom water

Method

Pulse walnuts in a food processor until they are the size of pine nuts, but make sure you don't grind them into a paste. Place the walnuts in a bowl and add cinnamon, sugar and nutmeg and mix well.

Place each pancake in your hand and fill it with one tablespoon of the walnut mixture. Fold over one side of the pancake onto the other, squeezing the edges together to seal into the shape of a half moon. Place the filled pancakes onto a baking tray and brush with butter on both sides. Bake on both sides until golden brown. In some cases the filled katayef are deep-fried in vegetable oil but this is a less healthy method.

While hot, dip into sugar syrup for 10 seconds coating both sides and place on a serving dish. Enjoy hot or cold. To enjoy them with the Arab cream ashta, place a tablespoon of ashta in the centre of the pancakes and bring the two sides together to make it look like a filled Italian cannoli, then drizzle with sugar syrup and enjoy.

Sugar syrup

Place sugar, water, lemon and orange blossom water in a saucepan on medium heat and cook for 5 to 7 minutes. Then allow it to cool for 5 minutes before dipping in the katayef.

Serves 10 people.

Yalanji (Warak enab bi-zayt) vegetable-filled vine leaves

Ingredients

- 2 brown onions
- 1 tbs salt
- ½ tsp ground pimento
- 4 small bunches flat-leaf parsley
- 3 large tomatoes
- 1 bunch fresh mint
- 1 cup washed medium-grain rice
- ½ cup extra virgin olive oil
- Juice of 2 lemons
- 1 potato, peeled and sliced
- 500g blanched vine leaves
- 1 cup water for cooking

Method

Chop the onions finely, add the salt and pimento and set aside. Wash and chop finely the parsley, tomatoes and mint leaves. Add the chopped ingredients to the washed and drained rice and mix well. Add the olive oil and lemon juice and mix. Place sliced potato in the bottom of a cooking pot to avoid the vine leaves sticking.

Take one leaf and place a tablespoon of the mixture in the centre of the bottom half then fold the sides in and begin to roll it to the top, sealing the filling in. Place it on top of the potato slices. Continue the process until all the leaves are filled. Place a heavy dish on top of the leaves to weigh them down while cooking. Pour the leftover dressing from the filling and a cup of water over the vine leaves, bring to the boil then reduce the heat to low, leaving a gentle simmer.

Cook for an hour or until the leaves are cooked. To test them take one out and taste it. If it's chewy then allow it to cook longer. When cooked, remove from heat and allow to cool completely. They are best served out of the fridge. Serve cold.

Serves 10 people.

Note: for blanching fresh vine leaves stack them into a neat pile and place in boiling water on the heat. Wait for their colour to change then remove and drain well. Use when cooled.

Moroccan chicken couscous

Ingredients

    4 large brown onions, chopped
    2 tbs vegetable oil
    1 whole chicken cut into 4 or 8 pieces, skinless
    2 tbs cumin, coarsely ground (for stock)
    ½ tsp ground cinnamon
    ½ tsp ground black pepper
    ½ tsp dried chilli flakes
    1 tsp sweet paprika
    2 tsp salt
    1.5 litres hot water
    2 × 400g cans chickpeas
    Zest of 1 lemon
    ground cumin

Ingredients for couscous

    1 × 500g box of couscous
    ¼ cup Italian parsley, washed and chopped roughly
    1 tsp ground dill seed
    chicken stock

Method

Sauté the onions in the vegetable oil on medium heat for 10 minutes or until they become translucent. Add the chicken pieces and brown for another 5 minutes. Add to the chicken all the spices, including the salt, and mix to release their aroma. Add hot water, cover and reduce the heat to low and cook for 30 minutes. When the chicken is cooked, add the drained and washed chickpeas, then half the lemon zest and mix and simmer for 5 minutes then set aside. Follow the cooking instructions on the couscous pack, this usually takes 10 minutes. The couscous tastes richer if you use the stock from the chicken instead of hot water.

When the couscous is ready toss it with chopped parsley and the remaining lemon zest with a dash of ground cumin.

Place the couscous on a large serving dish and arrange the chicken pieces on top. Pour the stock into a separate bowl to be drizzled over the chicken and couscous on each individual portion.

Serves 6 to 8 people.

Arwa's pesto paste

Ingredients

- 1 cup lightly toasted walnuts
- 2 garlic cloves
- 1 bunch fresh basil leaves
- ½ cup flat-leaf parsley
- ½ cup extra virgin olive oil
- ½ cup parmesan cheese
- Fresh cracked black pepper to taste
- 1 tsp salt (or to taste)
- Zest of 1 lemon

Method

Place the walnuts and garlic in a food processor and pulse a few times until in small bits (don't grind them to a powder). Add basil, parsley and olive oil and pulse until mixture forms a paste. Turn out mixture into a bowl and add parmesan cheese, pepper, salt, lemon zest and mix. If you like a bit of tang squeeze some lemon juice into the mix.

I enjoy the pesto on fresh Italian bread. You can also boil some spaghetti, mix in the pesto with a scoop of hot pasta water, toss well, drizzle with extra virgin olive oil and enjoy.

Chapter Six

A Sun-kissed Aussie

Slowly but surely Australia started to fit for me. Or me to it. Over the years my English had improved, I paid attention and listened extra hard, but I still wasn't free from my anxiety about making mistakes. I remember watching television with my parents and starting to understand the Australian colloquial terms that books don't teach you. We loved watching *Mother and Son* with Ruth Cracknell and Garry McDonald. We thought it was hilarious and as a family we'd watch *Hey Hey It's Saturday* and *All Together Now*. I was able to put the jokes into context and didn't feel so separate from it all. Australia was growing on me.

I started to immerse myself in Australian music, television and books and was a huge fan of the song 'Land Down Under' by the group Men at Work that both celebrated and laughed at Australian clichés. I loved songs by John Farnham like 'Burn For You' and 'You're the Voice' and Wendy Matthews might have been Canadian-born but her songs were so unpretentious, beautiful and timeless and seemed to embody what Australia was starting to mean to me, a sophisticated simplicity. What appears relaxed and laidback is in fact well thought out and assessed; Australians don't rush into things, we take our time. My mother always told me 'go slowly and you'll go well' so she was obviously more Aussie than she thought.

As its number of migrant students continued to grow Liverpool Girls' High planned a multicultural festival to showcase its diversity. I know it is hard to believe after having lived in Australia for more than a year and having someone like Annette dropping in with scones and Vegemite, but I had my first pavlova at one of these festivals, at the 'true blue Aussie' stand. I fell instantly in love with the crunchy shell with a soft marshmallow inside topped with berries and passionfruit pulp. It is my favourite dessert on a hot summer afternoon. At that festival I watched the dances of all the different cultures and tasted their foods and saw how the ones I knew had changed to accommodate the Aussie lifestyle, produce and tastebuds. Not much was like the original, it was a new version that combined the two creating a new beautiful and unique identity.

That's how I was starting to feel. I wasn't so much a teenager of two worlds but a person who was ready to embrace the best of these two worlds. It was a chance to belong on my own terms, though I still had a lot of years and some angst to go through before I would become the woman I wanted to be. By the time I was fifteen I'd lost my American accent and had begun to relax my R's. I sounded just like an Aussie kid. I had stopped being startled when the kookaburras started laughing, I knew what a southerly buster was, the way the billowing thunderclouds would roll in after a steamy summer day and bring relief from the heat that softened the bitumen roads and made us all listless and short-tempered. My hair would be sun-kissed and my face would be sunburned. There was a lot about Australia that I didn't seek, it just found me. I liked it, or most of it. Occasionally the dark side of human nature would show itself, but that ugliness can be found in any country.

Without even realising it Australia was now a part of me and my family, but some things changed in a way I didn't understand. As we got older the freedom that was so much a part of the fabric of an Australian childhood at the time wasn't something we were allowed. My mother started to limit where we went and she was very reluctant to let us out with friends to the park or even to walk to their homes for an afternoon. I resented it and when I pushed and asked that age-old teenager question 'why not?' my mother would say, 'I don't know their parents and what they do for a living.' It didn't make sense to me then. I understood my mother was doing her best, and of course she felt more comfortable with parents she knew well, but her unwillingness to let us go out alone wasn't just when visiting my friends' homes. She would only be happy if we went out together, with Reem or Maha.

It wasn't until years later my mother revealed what had shaped her opinion of our safety here in Australia and why she was so cautious. In 1986 we had just arrived in Australia for the first time when the Anita Cobby case rocked Australia and horrified the Australian public. I was too young and my parents protected us from knowing much but even with her limited English my mother was aware of what happened to this beautiful young woman. Anita Cobby was a nurse and one-time beauty queen who was walking home from Blacktown train station after a nightshift when she was abducted off the street by a group of men. She was raped repeatedly and slaughtered. The details of her murder were so horrific that the full details were suppressed. The five men responsible were caught and sentenced to life in prison, never to be released.

The whole country was shocked that something like this could happen. It wasn't the first time that a woman had been brutally murdered and it sadly wouldn't be the last, but the smiling photo of Anita that was published in newspapers and shown on the news tore at everyone's hearts, including my mother's. This murder shaped my mother's opinion about a woman's safety in Australia and as we got older it informed her decisions about what we could do. It wasn't religion that underpinned my parents' restrictions on us, it was fear. Because of our religion we had a chaperone or an adult with us when we were out when we were young, but this is what most parents do regardless of their religious affiliations.

Once we were mature enough to do things on our own we would be allowed some freedom, within the guidelines of our Islamic practices. I never expected my parents to allow me to go out to a nightclub with a group of my girlfriends as this was something that Islam forbade because it was a place associated with many sins. In fact, I am sure it isn't just Muslim parents who stop their daughters from going out to nightclubs. Through the years I would hear the same thing from girlfriends who weren't Muslim or Arab; their parents just didn't think it appropriate for them. I wasn't bothered by this restriction but I was not happy that I couldn't visit a friend's home or go to the park. Now I am an adult I can understand my mother's fear, but as a teenager I thought it too much.

After four years in Australia I had good friends and neighbours, familiar teachers and a routine. It was the longest I had spent in one place. In 1994 my father travelled to Saudi Arabia to pack our things and ship them down to Australia. Finally we were going to call one place home! When everything arrived it all looked so much smaller than I remembered, our lounges and beds. Our toys and Mum's kitchen things were all in boxes. Mostly they would stay there until my parents found the right house to buy and call our own a few years later.

I was learning every day about this new country we called home and one of the things that's strong in my memory is standing at school assembly during the minute's silence in respect for the fallen on Anzac Day. At first I wondered what it was all about and when I learned that Australia lost the Gallipoli campaign I was confused at what we were all celebrating, with a parade in the city, a public holiday and its own biscuit! Then I realised it was all in honour of the fallen soldiers who gave up their lives to fight for their country. Today I join in when my entire country is in silence for its fallen soldiers. My sadness for the lost lives of any soldiers or victim of war has only deepened as I've grown older.

By the time I was in Year Eleven, Reem was in Year Twelve studying for her HSC, and she convinced our mother to buy us a car. It was the moment a teenager dreams of. Having your very own car is a major step into adulthood. We became the proud owners of a 500-dollar, two-door 1976 Toyota Corolla. The car was the same age as I was! Finally, we were off the bus and Reem drove us both to school. The car had a bit of rust showing through, it was a faded sage green colour and every time it rained the water would drip onto my shoes through the dashboard but we loved it. By the end of Year Eleven I would get my licence just like my mother and sisters before me. Once Reem started studying a degree in visual arts at the University of New South Wales and Maha was studying biomedical science at the University of Technology, Sydney, I had the car to myself, as they both caught the train to the city.

I began to feel more independent and responsible but my parents were still reluctant to let me go out on my own with friends. They still preferred that my sisters and I were together if we went to the movies or shops as they knew we would look out for one another. The first time I spent a week away from my family was on a school camping trip in Year Eleven. I was lucky because Reem had crossed that bridge the year before and though my father was still reluctant he couldn't say no when Reem had come back safe and sound from her trip. I was so excited to be off with all my friends from school with a sleeping bag and late-night munchies packed, but I was a little scared at the same time. Even though I was with a group of people I knew well, at times I felt quite alone. During that trip I came to realise the safety and security my family unit provided me. I found being out in the world on my own was liberating but frightening at the same time. It made me appreciate the little things my parents did for me and I hoped I didn't take them for granted too much.

Some of the girls would say some awful things about their parents and it shocked me. I can honestly say my parents didn't understand everything I was going through, and in my mind they were over-protective, but I never felt that I hated them or that I needed to get away. As a parent today I think back and understand that my parents restricted us for (mostly) a good reason, but it was impossible for me to appreciate that then.

I might have been settling into Australia but it didn't mean I wanted to forget my heritage. In Year Twelve I was very proud to be voted a prefect by the students and teachers and to become a member of the school student council. I had picked up Arabic as one of my senior school electives but it wasn't offered during school hours so I had to attend lessons on a Saturday for four hours every weekend for two years. The level of Arabic that was being taught was easy for me as the level of education had been very high in Saudi Arabia. This gave me a big advantage and

A Sun-kissed Aussie

I was one of the top students. We always spoke Arabic at home with Mum and Dad; if they heard us speaking to each other in English my mother's voice would travel down the hall and she would say, 'Speak to each other in Arabic otherwise you'll forget it.' Mum knew we were speaking English at school and with friends so she was always trying to keep the equation balanced.

My youngest brother, Mohammad, though born in Australia, speaks Arabic extremely well due to the fact he heard us talking to him and each other in Arabic since he was a baby. He went to Arabic school briefly as a young boy and found it a waste of time in comparison to what he could learn from Mum, so every Saturday he would take out his Arabic books and Quran and take a lesson from her. I'm proud that he chose to learn Arabic and practise like he did with no pressure from any of us.

Liverpool and its surrounding suburbs now had many families from an Arabic-speaking background so teenagers would travel from a long way to attend the only school offering Arabic at HSC level in the area. The class had students with Iraqi, Assyrian, Kurdish and Lebanese backgrounds. The Iraqi kids were mostly Sunni Muslim, the Assyrians were Christians, and the Kurds were either Shia or Sunni Muslims, but there was no animosity among them. They were all humble people who got along. Some were sitting for their higher school certificates for the second time after graduating from Year Twelve in their homeland. The education system in Australia didn't recognise their certificate so they had to start from Year Eleven all over again. These kids had studied English back home and were extremely intelligent. I ran into one of the girls a few years ago and she had gone on to university and become a doctor. I was so proud of her because I remember how sad and frustrated she'd been when she discovered she couldn't go straight into university. I could relate to her being a proud student and I knew from experience it was hard to accept the knowledge you had didn't translate easily from one country to another.

I didn't mind spending my Saturdays learning about the Middle East and its history. It was fascinating to learn about ancient Mesopotamia, which is modern day Iraq, and is often referred to by historians as the 'cradle of civilisation'. This place was the epicentre of knowledge at the time and produced some of the greatest science, philosophy and poetry and it also inspired some of the most important developments in human history, including the invention of the wheel, the planting of the first cereal crops and the development of cursive script. These historical facts were absent from any discussion about Iraq during the time of the Gulf War.

In most cases the world was learning about Iraqis through the television news and all they could feel was resentment at why their sons and daughters were being sent there, along with their tax money. Most of the world only saw images of an angry dictator by the name of Saddam. These forgotten histories help us appreciate each other's existence and contributions to humanity, and acknowledging them keeps us connected to one another on the basis of our shared humanity.

I was proud of my heritage and enjoyed learning more. For my final Arabic oral exam I had to deliver a presentation in Arabic on a prominent Middle Eastern historical figure, Muslim or otherwise. I chose Saladin, better known in Arabic as Salah Al Din Al Ayoubi. Saladin was one of the most prolific and heroic Islamic leaders in the eleventh century. He possessed the skill of battle and diplomacy in war, and was well known for his kindness and extreme generosity to Muslims and non-Muslims alike. Saladin was actually not Arab but was in fact Kurdish-born in the city of Takrit in Iraq. He led the Muslims against the Crusaders and eventually recaptured Palestine from the Crusader Kingdom. He is respected for being a true Muslim who promoted the idea that respecting all Muslims, Christians and Jews could live peacefully in the holy land and especially in Jerusalem. This is also what Islam teaches. As an Australian teenager with an Arab heritage I felt an immediate respect for this man who, though he'd lived centuries before me, seemed to think as I did that what mattered was our similarities not our differences.

I made good friends in those Arabic classes and after our final exam one of the girls in the class, Lena, invited us home to celebrate. We all had to travel to Birrong to sit the exam. It was lovely to get together afterwards and not rush off back home because we probably wouldn't see each often once school was over. We had the most mouth-watering meal of *Quzi* – it's pronounced similar to Aussie – which is roasted lamb spiced with an array of Middle Eastern spices: cinnamon and pimento, black pepper and nutmeg. The baby lamb is dry rubbed in the spice mix inside and out, stuffed with a mixture of rice, mince and nuts. It's then slow roasted for six hours for perfect melt in your mouth meat. My mother makes this classic Arab dish but we have put a bit of Aussie into the *Quzi* we make. I finely chop some fresh rosemary leaves and add them to the dry spice mix with some olive oil as I coat the baby lamb's skin. The rosemary perfumes the meat, giving it an aroma and flavour like no other. I love making this for my family on holidays when we all get together and spend all day enjoying each other's company. Even if it's not a whole baby lamb I use the same spice mix for a leg of lamb roast.

That day I enjoyed the delicious lamb, laughing and chatting in English and Arabic with my friends. We had a wonderful time. I only wish all my school experiences had been as lovely.

* * *

Sadly, bullying and ridicule happens in schools all over the world. Up until Year Twelve I had never really experienced much of it directly, apart from the usual whispered words and some unfriendliness on the bus. I had earned the respect of my fellow students and the teachers and the school counsellor would call upon me often to help translate for Arabic-speaking parents. I was proud that I was helping bridge the two worlds in a way that didn't leave someone being misunderstood or frustrated because they didn't speak English or Arabic. But then something happened and for the first time I was in a situation where I was the brunt of some of my classmates' prejudice.

I didn't see it coming at all. I was sitting at my desk waiting for the teacher to arrive and some Muslim girls walked in with a girl of Fijian Islander heritage and her Aussie friends. They were arguing and it was quite heated so everyone else went quiet. I had no idea what it was about and wasn't going to get involved until the Fijian girl stood up and shouted, 'You fucken Muslim bitches.' It was as if she had leaned over and slapped me and something in me stirred. It wasn't my fight but what she said deeply offended me. We were classmates and I had known this girl for a long time. There had never been any animosity between us before that day, but I wasn't going to let her insult my religion. I turned and said, 'Don't swear at my religion, Islam has nothing to do with your fighting!' She came at me, stood beside my chair and threatened to hit me if I spoke again.

This girl was a well-known troublemaker and I was a prefect, so I had a lot to lose, but I wasn't going to be intimidated. I think the unspoken prejudices I'd felt and seen, especially since my friendship with Abeer, had stirred a lot of emotions that were now coming to the surface. I didn't realise the anger I felt about it until that moment. I stood up and said again, 'Don't swear at my religion. How would you like it if I said that about yours?' She made a swing at my face with her fist and my natural instinct was to move back as I saw it coming. She missed me and I gathered my fingers into a fist and swung back. I punched her in the face and I think it shocked me more than her that we had somehow ended up in a physical fight. She was furious and swung at me again, and missed again. I punched her once more just as the teacher walked into the room.

We were both sent to the office and even though the principal knew me and my excellent school record she still had to punish us both. She apologetically said to me, 'I have to suspend you for hitting her even though she started the fight.' I was suspended for one day and my mother wasn't happy about that, but when I explained exactly what had happened she was glad I stood up for myself. My parents had always taught us that aggression and violence is never a solution to anything, but they'd also taught us to protect ourselves. It is not in the true Muslim to be the aggressor, but when in harm you must protect yourself as human nature prevails whether you are Muslim or not. I felt so bad afterwards that from that day I knew aggression was not for me. And once I went back to school I resolved to never hit anyone again. I eventually spoke with that girl again and even though we never became good friends we weren't enemies either.

When you are a teenager, school is a huge part of your life and any confrontation or bullying can have a huge impact on you. I was lucky, I had a strong connection to my sisters that gave me a buffer and enough of a sense of my identity that I was not too severely affected by this incident. But I will always remember the shock I felt to suddenly go from getting ready for a class to being verbally and then physically attacked. Bullies look for any point of difference to exploit and my religion was an easy target. I couldn't believe how quickly a situation could change. I was determined to move on and focus on doing well at school.

For my HSC I completed 3-unit Arabic, 3-unit Legal studies, 2-unit maths, English, Economics and Visual Art. I'd been inspired by Reem when I picked Art as one of my HSC subjects. She is a naturally gifted artist and I think she is brilliant. This view wasn't only a little sister's belief though, she was among the top students in the state and her final HSC work was selected for the Art Express exhibition.

Once Reem was at university I'd help her out and she taught me so many new things, especially in photography. I was never much of a painter and I can't draw well but photography is something I enjoy immensely. As with my studies in Arabic, I focused hard on my art studies and learned about the way women artists have been treated over the years; it was a real eye-opener for me. The fact that some women had to sign the name of a man, such as their father or husband, because a woman wasn't entitled to claim the work as her own was appalling to me. This was also the case in literature and in ownership of property. Again the influence of the strong women I knew was at work on my perceptions of life. All these things I was learning in school, and all the things I'd seen in my life – like Hindiya teaching herself through books, Annette driving us to Sydney, and my mother earning a driver's licence on her own – were starting to build my picture of the world.

I began my search, a search for equality and justice; but where would it be? In God's rules or manmade rules? This search would take me on a journey of self discovery beyond my wildest expectation.

A Sun-kissed Aussie

As Year Twelve came to an end I realised that things were changing again. My school graduation ceremony was a month away and for any teenager this is a huge stepping stone, marking the move away from the world of a child out into that of an adult. Out of the blue, a note came to me in class from the Year Twelve music teacher asking to see me at lunchtime. I didn't take music as an elective but my friend Anna did; she played bass guitar. The guitar in all its variations is my favourite instrument and I enjoyed listening to her many times. I like to listen to all kinds of music, both classical and modern, but my most beloved music is traditional Arabic. It has an old-world charm in its rhythms and verses, and seems to me more like poetry than a dance beat.

I truly adore listening to the Arab *oud* (guitar), *kanun* (string instrument) and the Arab flute. They can take you on a magical carpet ride into another time and link you to the past. Music can be an escape and during the stress of the HSC I liked to relax listening to these pure sounds. Music can become a means to link one culture to the other, just like food. Many musicians today have created music that links cultures together, people like Sting who has written songs that have verses entirely in Arabic intertwined into an English song. It is so beautiful, a combination of two different artistic and cultural expressions coming together in musical harmony. And it is not only the music that can link people. Lyrics can often describe emotions and aspirations that people struggle to articulate themselves but can share through a song.

Anna had told the music teacher that I had a good voice, she'd listened to me sing to myself at lunchtime or during our free periods. I didn't think I was that good, but I could carry a tune. Singing to me was a stress relief, a way to get it all out. I didn't know what this teacher wanted and I was surprised when he asked me to sing the Year Twelve farewell song at our final assembly. The music class of that year had only five students and none of them was a singer.

'I'd like you to sing "Whatever". It's a song by Oasis, I'm sure you've heard it.' I *had* heard the song and liked it, but I wasn't confident enough in my singing to perform in front of the whole school, the parents and teachers, and I told him so. He asked me to think about it and gave me a tape of the song. 'There is no one else to do it and I'm told you have a great voice. If you don't, we'll have to get one of the Year Eleven girls to do it.' He wanted me to let him know the next day.

I went home and listened to the song over and over and over again. The message of the lyrics meant a lot to me, telling us we are all free to be whoever we want to be. I talked it over with Mum and decided to do it.

For the next four weeks I practised either with the band or by myself every day. As nervous as I was, I felt a huge weight come off my shoulders when I started singing, because every time I sang my heart out and lost myself in the moment.

I stood up the day of my graduation and looked out on a hall full of people, I was nervous but I gathered myself and took the microphone and started to sing. I sang for all the days past, and for those coming, for all the good times and bad, and halfway through the song I realised a great many of my fellow Year Twelve students were in tears. All I could see was girls hugging each other. They were all seated in alphabetical order, not near their friends, but they still hugged whoever was right next to them. I saw Arab girls who had been rivals with the Australian girl next to them embrace in a moment of raw human emotion. It was a turning point for all of us as we all realised we were growing up. We weren't teenagers anymore. The responsibility of adult life dawned on us in the ceremony and we all realised we were forever linked. We were mates and no matter how different they thought we were, we shared much that was the same.

Years later I was invited back to visit Liverpool Girls' High as a guest speaker at their Harmony Day school assembly. As I looked out into the crowd of students I flashed back to when I was up on that same stage conducting the school assembly as a prefect in Year Twelve. It was as if no time had passed and yet so much had changed. I had Lamya, my four-year-old daughter with me. She saw her mum give a speech and all the girls in the school 'oohed' and 'aahed' at the little girl who was so brave and well behaved. I wanted them all to see a mother who was proud of who she was and someone teaching her child the courage of standing in front of an audience and sharing her experiences.

Aussie pavlova with a hint of Mediterranean topping

Ingredients for base

- 10 egg whites
- 1 tsp cream of tartar
- 2½ cups caster sugar
- 1 tsp vanilla bean paste

Ingredients for topping

- 600ml pure cream whipped with 2 tbs of caster sugar and some lemon zest
- 1 punnet of strawberries, halved
- 1 punnet of blueberries
- 4 passionfruit pulp
- 1 cup of fresh de-seeded cherries, don't discard any juice that is a result of the de-seeding.
- Seeds of one pomegranate, don't discard any juice that is a result of the de-seeding.
- 1 tsp orange blossom water
- Zest of half a lemon or lime
- Some crushed pistachio nuts

Method

Preheat fan-forced oven to 130°C. Line a large baking sheet with baking paper. Beat egg whites and cream of tartar in a large bowl with an electric mixer until light and fluffy. Gradually add sugar while beating continuously. Continue beating until mixture is stiff and glossy. This should take about 10 minutes. Add vanilla bean paste at the very end of the beating process. Spread mixture on to prepared sheet and shape into a large dome (it should look like a cake).

Place the pavlova into the oven and immediately reduce the temperature to 100°C. Cook for 45 minutes or until it is firm to the touch. Turn off the oven and allow the pavlova to cool in the oven for a few hours with the door closed.

Decorate with the whipped cream and fruit, drizzle with the juice from the pitted cherries and pomegranate mixed with the orange blossom water. Sprinkle the lemon zest and pistachio nuts to finish.

Serves up to 10 people.

Chapter Seven

The University of Life

My parents encouraged all their children to finish their studies and continue to university. They regarded education very highly and we had two choices – study or work – no daughter of theirs was going to sit at home awaiting a Prince Charming to come knocking on her door. We had to have a career, and marriage was not a career in my parents' eyes. That didn't mean they didn't want us to find the right man and be happy but they made it clear it wasn't what our life should be focused on. Independence and personal success happens away from being reliant on others. My parents knew we would make better choices if we were well informed about the world and what kind of people were in it.

As a young woman, I never saw marriage as an immediate goal. I always pictured myself with a degree or two, in a good job in a career I enjoyed. I never imagined myself with kids, that was way off in the future. I wasn't looking to rush into anything. For me finding the right person to share my life with meant finding my soul mate, just anyone wasn't going to do.

Once I finished my HSC I spotted my first grey hair and was horrified. But I knew why I had it, I'm not a screamer or a fighter – I bear my pain in silence and it affects me greatly. When anything gets too much one or two pop out.

I was so proud the day I received my HSC results in the mail. My parents' dreams of empowering us with our right to be educated was finally accomplished, all three of their daughters had achieved an education and it was now up to us. Maha and Reem were already at university, but I watched how tired they were after travelling to the city every day and that commute was a big deterrent to me. Whenever I did go into the city with Reem I would notice how no one acknowledges anybody around them, how you would get pushed in the avalanche of people all crossing the street at the same time and not even one 'sorry' would be said. Everyone was in a hurry to be somewhere else, rushing along oblivious to others. I knew I wasn't a city girl. I decided to go to the University of Western Sydney, in Milperra. I would catch the bus to Liverpool station and get on another bus from there to uni so it would only take forty minutes. On the days I drove the Corolla it was even quicker.

My first day at university, in 1996, was an adrenalin rush. My friend Abeer and I were studying the same degree, a Bachelor of Social Science, and it was lovely to have a familiar face among the new people and teachers. The University of Western Sydney was just the right size for me; it wasn't so big that I would get lost in identical corridors. I loved being there. But there were some things I was puzzled by.

I walked down the tree-lined path many times to get to my car and quite a few times there'd be a strange smell, unfamiliar and heavy in the air. I'd already struggled to understand the bar on campus and how drinking alcohol was part of university life, but one day I was with one of my friends and I commented on this strange smell. She told me that it was from the students

The University of Life

smoking marijuana nearby. Addictive substances are all forbidden in Islam, and drugs and alcohol fall into this category. For me, it was an education in what other people were up to.

Marijuana is a natural substance that has some medicinal uses that are beneficial to humans but as a recreational activity it is prohibited in Islam.

Having Abeer at university with me made everything so much easier. It was like coming to Australia, then I had my sisters to share things with, now I had Abeer. I was surprised to find that she was one of only two or three veiled women at the University of Western Sydney when we were only five minutes from Bankstown, which has a high Arab population. My first year of study taught me a lot about how people really felt about certain issues. The many tutorial discussions would be fuelled with differences of opinion and I was introduced to how people could have such different understandings of the same point. Freedom of opinion was encouraged and yet it seemed that political correctness was something people understood but only applied to their own rights, not to others'. I would sit and listen to some terribly ignorant comments from fellow students about immigration and often their ideals and opinions were based on something far from reality; these were opinions based on a complete dismissal of what migrants have contributed to Australia. The fact is migrants are a vital element in Australia's existence. But I listened and tried to share what I knew from experience, hoping they might understand and think of things from another viewpoint.

The fact she was a minority didn't deter Abeer, she was always proud and down to earth. There was a very small number of Arabic-speaking students at the university and they would get together between lessons. It was like me in high school; they were drawn together by their ethnicity. Some of them were the first in their families to reach university-level education so there was a lot of pressure on them to make their family proud. To be the first in your family to strive for higher goals than the ones set by your parents wasn't simply a migrant issue; many Australian students were doing the same. There was just an added poignancy for the children whose parents were war refugees – people from places where the biggest concern was staying alive, not getting an A.

Abeer and I would sit with this group occasionally and we'd all have some laughs and have a good time. I remember one of the guys, Michael Kanaan, was in my criminology class. He was always so polite and I noticed he was unwilling to participate in jokes that were offensive, especially to women. He was a high distinction student and he didn't say much in class. I always felt he was sitting back taking it all in and I could never tell what he was thinking. I didn't see Michael much after my first year, and during 1997 he would be absent quite often. But when I did see him he always said hello.

By 1998, Michael was never in class. One night I was sitting watching the news with my parents. Over the previous few weeks there'd been a number of Sydney shootings and the media were speculating that there was some sort of Kings Cross drug war going on. I sat in disbelief as they talked about Michael Kanaan. I thought it was another Michael Kanaan, but when they showed his photograph I felt my face turn white. I gasped and said without thinking, 'He was at uni with me!' Both my parents had concern on their faces. I could see them thinking, *How could our daughter know this man!* I knew they were concerned that someone like that had been at university with their daughter.

Though we were all still living under the same roof, my family and I were all busy with our own things. Firas, seventeen, and Mohammad, ten, were both still at school. Mohammad was into

The University of Life

soccer, and he would have a game every Saturday morning at the park at the end of our street. I would often walk down with him and watch him play. I remember he was feeling left out of the family because he was the youngest and everyone else was busy with their own lives. I did my best to do things with him. I took him to a soccer match at Parramatta Stadium when Mark Bosnich was at the beginning of his career and was the main attraction. He has never forgotten that and always reminds me of how much he appreciated it.

Maha and Reem used to catch up on their sleep every Sunday but I couldn't. An early bird, I was always up and ready to make the Sunday family breakfast with Mum. We'd prepare an array of different breakfast dishes popular in the Middle East. Hot fava beans that the Arabs call *foul*: semi-mashed with lemon juice, salt and garlic with a dash of vinegar and tahina topped with olive oil and fresh parsley. A plate of *labneh*, drizzled with extra virgin olive oil; a plate of *za'atar*, haloumi cheese and three different types of olives; a vegetable platter filled with cut tomatoes, cucumbers and shallots. A fresh bunch of parsley, mint and oregano leaves from Mum's herb garden with some boiled eggs: it was mouth-watering. It was the perfect breakfast after a week of coffee and cafeteria food.

One morning as we were working together my mother put something different on the table. She'd discovered Danish blue cheese, not a hugely popular cheese in the Middle East. I took a bite and fell in love with it. Later when Maha, Reem, Firas and Mohammed joined us they all let Mum know they didn't share my love and we couldn't convince them to try again. Nowadays, Mum and I often share a cup of tea with some blue cheese and honey on some crackers for a snack. My three children love it too.

My parents were so proud their three girls were all at university and now it was time to make another dream come true and they started to think about buying their own home. They found a brand new display home that was for sale. The house was picture perfect with a peach paint finish. The yard was filled with native Australian plants to withstand the summer heat but it was a garden created for low maintenance and there was no benefit to the dinner table.

Most Arab homes in Australia have a plant or two that will add to the dinner table. Their homes are more like the traditional Australian quarter acre block used to be, with fruit trees or vegie gardens. But it didn't have to be a quarter acre, you'd be amazed at how much can grow in the smallest spaces. Probably the most common plant you'd find would be a basil plant. Basil is one of the heavenly things God has mentioned in the Quran. Its medicinal benefits are remarkable and science has proved it has properties that help relax blood vessels for better blood flow and is a natural anti-inflammatory. Its aroma alone is refreshing and sweet, and basil is an ingredient in many of the foods cooked in the Middle East. Now I am married and have a family of my own the food that it's mostly used for in my own kitchen is the Aussie favourite, the humble sausage roll. I learned to make healthy, tasty sausage rolls from an unlikely source: my mother-in-law Amal.

Amal would never have seen or eaten a sausage roll in her life before she came to Australia. It is not a familiar food in Lebanon. But being the woman she is, she found a way to make this Aussie favourite at home for her kids who craved it at school but who didn't eat it because it wasn't Halal. She combines fine lean lamb mince with onions and fresh basil and a bunch of other ingredients with a few sheets of puff pastry. The smell of them cooking would reach the street and her children would come running.

The University of Life

My mother-in-law Amal is a proud, strong and resilient woman. No matter what she was faced with she managed to make the best of the situation. I regard her as a hero; she unselfishly let go of any dreams she had that would force her to be away from raising her children in this new place. I don't know if that was fair, but to her it was the right thing to do. All of her children, especially my husband Hazem, are upstanding people with high morals and kind hearts.

Amal never spoke any English but she would still make sure she was informed about her children's issues at school and in their personal lives. Like Hindiya, she is another self-educated woman who has taught me that decorum and class is something that comes from within, not from an institution.

My parents bought their first house in Hinchinbrook, a few suburbs west of Liverpool. After so many years of never having their own home it must have been an amazing feeling for them to have the safety and stability of owning the roof over our heads. Reem sewed curtains for our room that matched our bedspreads. I loved the feeling that owning our home gave me. I felt it was a final assurance that we weren't going anywhere – we were going to be in Australia for a long time. I could finally take out all my things from their boxes. My mother was so excited she planted a herb garden in the backyard along with lemon and guava trees and a grapevine that travelled up the pergola. That grapevine came from a branch she took with her from that old haunted house we lived in. In spring it would be at its peak, carrying grapes so sweet and fragrant dangling above our heads. The leaves would cover the top of the pergola, creating a shady space underneath. It was the perfect place to enjoy the cool summer evening breeze during our family barbecues. My father would pick the grapes and put them in a bowl of ice – the perfect summer dessert.

We spent so many beautiful times under that grapevine. My sisters and I would bring out some mats and lay them on the ground with some thin cushions to sit on; my father would light the barbecue with some coal and he would sit on the floor beside it and cook the meat that was spiced with Mum's special mix. Mum would prepare the salad and hummus; simple food, nothing fancy. As we all sat on the ground talking and laughing I couldn't help but remember Saudi Arabia and saw the Arab in me sitting in the way of the prophet in my Aussie backyard. Dad would pull the meat from the barbecue into a pocket of Arab bread to keep it hot. The bread would be soaked with the juices from the meat, perfect to dip in the garlic dip my mother made.

After our first year of university, Abeer transferred to Sydney University to study a degree in Orthoptics. The long summer holidays began and Reem and I found some casual work. I got a job in a clothing store and it would teach me a thing or two about being independent and dealing with customers. I would work for many businesses over the years, mostly women's clothing, and what I would experience as a young woman dealing with the wandering eyes of some male customers was unbelievable.

A man and his wife would be shopping for some clothes and while she was in the change room he would attempt to flirt with me or one of my colleagues. Not all the men would be so bold, but most of the single ones would be checking out all the girls on the floor as if that's what we were there for. I would feel so degraded and I knew some of my colleagues felt the same way.

After a few years Reem got me a job at her work. It was in home furnishings and I was far less likely to have to deal with wayward husbands there. Reem taught me what she knew, and I learned the craft of making curtains. Both my mother and grandmother Hindiya had sewn simple clothes, so I guess the

The University of Life

skill runs in the family. It was another creative avenue for Reem and she was good at it. She was so talented she would end up designing and sewing her own wedding dress.

I found the second year at university tough. I missed Abeer and I was confused about what I should be studying and what I should major in. Towards the end of first year I was really starting to question some of what I was learning and what I wasn't. I had enrolled in history and at the first lecture we were told what the subject 'European History' covered. When the lecturer got to the timeline where Europe was the cradle for the Islamic empire he skipped 800 years of history and civilisation. I put my hand up and asked, 'What about the time of the Islamic empire in Europe? The Moors?' and he replied, 'No, no, we don't cover that part, we do before and after that time.' I walked to the office and dropped 'European History' that same day. I began to feel angry that university was not providing me with the opportunities to learn what I had come to uni to find – where was my place in this world; where was my place in this multicultural society that doesn't know much about me? I was disillusioned that it seemed no one was interested in Middle Eastern culture unless it was the bad stuff.

At the time nearly any Arab on TV was portrayed negatively. And in news reports it seemed I was always hearing the words 'Middle Eastern' or 'Lebanese' and not so many descriptions of other ethnicities. It was frustrating and unfair in my eyes. No matter where criminals come from, their mistakes fall on them alone, not on an entire region of the world. Where did this resentment toward the Arab Australians come from and why? I am pleased that this has started to change; recently the television show *East West 101* is depicting a proud, honest Arab Australian.

In my second year I took English as one of my electives. At first, I had dreaded walking into class because I still felt I wasn't as good at it as everyone else. The first lecture was on Classic American literature and our teacher was the accomplished poet and writer Peter Skrzynecki. He looked around the room and asked us to tell him our names and where we were from. I was really nervous. When I was in high school with Abeer one of our male teachers, who we respected greatly, said to her, 'Abeer, you know every time I'm at the pub ordering a beer I think of your name.' He meant it to be funny but for any girl, especially a veiled Muslim girl, to hear from her male teacher that her name reminded him of alcohol was confronting and offensive.

'Arrrwa.' Peter Skrzynecki attempted to sound out the 'r'. 'What does it mean?' he asked, and with all my courage I replied, 'It means satisfaction, like when you drink water and you're not thirsty anymore.' He said, 'That feeling is called quenched thirst, so your name means quenched thirst. Very nice, I haven't heard that before.' He moved on to the next student but from that day I knew the right way to explain my name in English, it was an exact translation to the meaning I already knew in Arabic. I decided then and there that I liked this teacher. He understood me and I was determined to give the class a go. Peter would become a mentor to me during my university studies and since I graduated he and his family have remained close family friends.

Having a teacher like Peter Skrzynecki, who encouraged me but also recognised the influence of my religion and culture, meant I focused even harder on my learning. By reading the work of writers who expressed history and cultural events through fiction I was introduced to wide-ranging and fascinating issues – tragedy and war, love and hate, fathers and daughters, mothers and sons, relationships as old as time.

My passion for literature was unearthed and I started reading writers like Judith Wright, Edgar Allan Poe, Mrs Aeneas Gunn,

The University of Life

Raymond Carver, David Malouf, Barbara Baynton and Katherine Mansfield, and many more. My absolute favourite was Janet Frame, her autobiography *An Angel at My Table* changed me forever. She is such a raw and unpretentious writer and poet: I truly love her work. She had written perfectly about being in a world that categorises people and when you are different you can be completely overlooked in life just because you don't fit the mould. I loved her honesty and shameless truths about issues that are at once so personal and universal. I cried and laughed at the same time at some of the things that related to me.

All these new ideas and new discoveries added to my confusion about who I was, and what defined me as a person. Was it the way I looked, the country I came from, my religion or what I wore? What mould was I supposed to fit into? I wasn't sure and I was looking for answers. I was ready to explore all this and I didn't realise that the next chapter in my life was just around the corner. It would reveal to me much more about myself than I knew.

Foul with tahina

Ingredients

- 2 × 450g cans of foul (fava or broad beans), drained and rinsed well
- ½ cup lemon juice
- 2 tbs apple vinegar
- 1 tsp salt
- 2 garlic cloves, crushed
- 3 tbs extra virgin olive oil
- 1 tbs tahina
- ¼ cup Italian parsley, finely chopped

Method

Place the drained and washed foul in a saucepan and top with water until covered. Bring to the boil and then simmer for 10 minutes.

In a mixing bowl add all the ingredients except the tahina and parsley. Mix with a whisk until it emulsifies. Drain the foul and add it to the dressing. With a fork mix the foul well while crushing some of them with the back of the fork. Add tahina and mix well. If the mix appears dry add 2 tablespoons of hot water. Pour into a serving dish and top with chopped parsley and drizzle with extra virgin olive oil. Serve with Arab bread and fresh tomato, cucumbers and shallots.

Serves 4 people.

Labneh

Labneh is a thick yoghurt that you can find at any Middle Eastern grocer ready to eat. Easy to make, I have made labneh at home many times. It is plain yoghurt that has been salted to taste and has been drained overnight in a cheesecloth (muslin). This drains the liquid and produces a thick rich spreadable yoghurt, just like cream cheese. Place a portion in a semi-flat plate and drizzle with extra virgin olive oil. Toast some Arab bread and dip it in the labneh; enjoy it with fresh mint, olives and cut Lebanese cucumbers.

Za'atar

Za'atar is an oregano mix sold at most Middle Eastern grocers. It is a mix of dried oregano leaves, sumac, sesame seeds, dried coriander, salt and cumin and many other spices; the mix varies from one country to the other. To serve, place some za'atar in a small dish with extra virgin olive oil in another dish. Toast some Arab bread and dip it in the oil then into the za'atar. Enjoy with a cup of tea.

Amal's sausage rolls

Ingredients

- 1 large brown onion, grated
- 2 slices white sliced bread, trimmed of crust, soaked in cold water and squeezed to remove excess water
- 2 tsp Italian mixed herbs
- 1 tsp ground black pepper
- 1 tsp ground cinnamon
- 1 tsp ground pimento
- 1 tsp salt
- 1kg extra fine lean mince
- ½ bunch fresh basil leaves washed and chopped finely
- 4 to 6 sheets of puff pastry
- 1 egg, beaten, for egg wash

Method

Place grated onion and soaked bread in a large bowl with all the dried spices. Using your hands mash them well until they are combined. Add the meat and freshly chopped basil leaves and mix well using your hands.

Cut each pastry sheet into two pieces lengthways and line a row of the meat mix down the middle of each. Roll the pastry over the mix and turn it over, keeping the overlapping sides facing down. Cut into 2 or 3 pieces and place on a greased baking sheet. Using a fork, press down on the top of each sausage roll to make a pattern and brush with some egg wash. Bake for 15 to 20 minutes or until golden brown.

Makes approximately 18 pieces.

Chapter Eight
The Year of El Magic

I can't say that things were all rosy for me during my second year of university. Abeer had moved to Sydney University and I didn't socialise very much with my classmates. I was immersed in my part-time work and I was enjoying it but life at home was so dysfunctional. Dad would be off for months at a time and my siblings and I were all young adults trying to find our own way in life. We were working and studying so hard that we were too busy for our traditional Sunday breakfasts.

Firas and Mohammad were still at school and Reem and Maha were like me, juggling university and paid work. The only person who seemed content was Mum. Finally, after years of devoting herself to her family and supporting my father in his career she had found something she enjoyed and was ready for a change. She was in her forties and was blossoming in her job as a floristry teacher. The lessons were run by the TAFE for migrant women. She taught her first class in mid 1995, the year I was sitting for my HSC, and by 1997 she was confident and proud of her skills. She became a floristry teacher in programs run especially for migrant women who didn't speak English well, or at all. During classes, my mother would signal to the students what to do; there were often few words spoken, it was all in the body language. I never knew how much my mother loved flowers until she started doing this. I remember my father always buying her flowers: I guess without knowing he encouraged in her the natural artist she was to become. I have been stopped in the street by many who tell me, 'Your mother was my teacher and I have my own floristry shop thanks to her.' Some of these women were from war-torn countries, like Iraq, and were in deep depression from what they had witnessed during the war. These women found a way to express themselves without words just like Mum did. Mum is still teaching today; like many Australian women she continues to work well into her sixties.

When I arrived home from university late in the evening I would walk through the front door and the smell of a spring garden permeated the house. I would see my mother standing at the dining table with bunches of flowers, concentrating hard. She would be in her own world, arranging a vase with an artistic sensibility, oblivious to an argument Reem and Firas were having about him wanting to borrow her car and her saying no.

Through flowers, Mum discovered a passion and artistic skill she never knew she had. She would spend hours drawing her own diagrams and photographing her designs to share with her students. She read everything she could find about flowers native to Australia, from the crimson waratah to the golden wattle with a few bottlebrushes in between. Mum would create an arrangement full of natives and it would be the centrepiece of our dinner table for weeks. She would research where the best quality and best priced flowers were available locally for her students to help them save a few dollars. Mum ran her class in English, but if there was someone who spoke only Arabic she would translate the lesson as she went along so they wouldn't feel left out.

The Year of El Magic

She would pair up any woman who was a new arrival from a range of different countries with a student who spoke English better and who would translate for her and look after her so she wouldn't feel isolated and give up. Mum encouraged all her students and helped them build female networks with each other. Mum was doing something new and enjoyable, but she really hadn't ventured far from what she'd been doing for us all her life. She was, in my eyes and in the eyes of many of her students, a mother to them, guiding and encouraging them, teaching them a skill and helping them fit in. It was a powerful message to have my mother, Asmaa, a migrant who had found her place in her new country helping others do the same.

My mother faced great challenges teaching for TAFE. She'd taken the class herself and was then recommended by her first floristry teacher, who was retiring and had been asked to find a qualified replacement for her position. She approached my mother as she knew she had been a teacher in Saudi Arabia and she considered my mother her most talented student. Mum was the only candidate for the job. She was so excited and she told my father about the offer. At first they were both unsure about the work environment she would be in and hesitant about how she was going to fill the requirements of class schedule reports and all the paperwork, which was all in English. She needed to be tested and have her degree evaluated and translated to English so she could then be interviewed by TAFE.

Although Mum's English had improved significantly by then I still remember my sisters and I telling her we would help her with all the written parts as much as we could until she was confident to do it by herself. We told her she needn't worry about making sure there was dinner on the table every night, we were all happy to pitch in and help make things work. My father told her that he knew she could do it. We all felt it was our turn to help our mother and support her in pursuing her dream. My sisters and I became our mother's female support network.

Women all over the world throughout history have supported each other and so we were just continuing this age-old practice. The female experience is shared across countries and religions; she is predetermined by creation to be the vessel of life. Though some women, by choice or fate, do not have children, for many becoming the source of sustenance for a child or a family is a burdensome privilege. I am sure it was for my mother. It is a sacrificial role no matter how you look at it. A mother's mind, body and soul, her whole life, becomes consumed in this nurturing role if she chooses to take it. It was only fair that we repaid my mother for her selflessness.

My mother was finding new satisfaction but I can remember being so depressed and overworked staying on top of my uni work and trying to make sure I didn't fall behind in my English reading. I'm not a fast reader and every week we would have a new novel that we were meant to finish for the following week. I found with working, studying and helping out at home there was no time for anything else. When things got too hard I never walked away. I would shrug off anything that was unfriendly and unwelcoming, but that doesn't mean it didn't hurt and the feeling of rejection made me cry many times. I felt like everything I did was always twice the effort of others around me, but I had a greater goal – survival. And I also wanted to prove that people's minds can be changed with kindness and knowledge rather than through frustration and anger.

It is common for migrants to feel frustrated while constantly trying to fit in. You can miss your children growing up and precious moments with family and friends. Finding the time and enthusiasm to take up surfing or cricket can be impossible. A father who is frustrated at not being able to work in his profession and a mother who doesn't understand the language well and children always playing catch-up in class work that they don't really understand, is continuously demanding. Everyone ends up swimming in their own problems . . . and that frustration has to go somewhere.

In some cases frustration can be directed at parents by the children who are finding this new place far too difficult to settle into, especially when bound by a culture and traditions that were invisible to most people around them. Or it would be directed at the kids by their parents, who had sacrificed everything to bring their family to a place that was safe and with far more opportunities than where they were. They want to give them the opportunity to pursue their dreams but then become angry at children who seem ungrateful.

Normality is not in the equation for any migrant in the early days of settling in. I remember an Anglo-Australian teacher at a special education school I worked for while I was at university; she was a very loud and dominating character which made her racist attitude towards me even more visible. One day the staff held a morning-tea party and everyone brought a plate. I decided to bring some falafel, crisp and green, that my mother and I had made much earlier that morning. They were gone in seconds. Everyone was asking me how to make them as they found them tasty and wished there were more. I shared the complicated recipe willingly.

This particular woman seemed to wait for the opportunity to humiliate me. She steered the conversation around so she could ask me what my favourite Cold Chisel song was. I told her I didn't know who they were. She laughed and said, 'Where the hell have you been? What do you mean you have never heard of Cold Chisel? What rock have you been hiding under?' I was embarrassed and felt inadequate, as though I wasn't Australian enough. She implied that a true blue Aussie was defined by their knowledge of Cold Chisel songs. I knew she had grabbed the opportunity to put me down. All the other teachers looked at her, but said nothing to defend me, and neither did I. I wish I had told her I was too busy trying to fit in to tick off a knowledge of every rock band, but I don't think she would have understood anyway.

That woman reminds me that certain people will always judge you according to their own standards instead of trying to relate to you and learn about you and your differences. She lived in her own world, oblivious to anyone else around her, and perhaps found my presence in her country confronting. Perhaps she was one of those people who ate a kebab but didn't know where it came from.

'Assimilation' is a word I don't like and in many cases it is used by some to destroy cultural diversity. Why can't we coexist and love and respect each other's differences and learn from them instead of moulding them into something that we only tolerate? 'Tolerate' is another awful word that implies a lack of cohesion and an animosity between groups. These words imply that we are not meant to get along, when the truth is far from that. But those moments when I was made to feel small and insignificant were not going to change me. I was determined to stay positive and optimistic even though I was struggling. But my confidence was dented and during that second year of university going out with friends or even as a family was not a part of my weekend plans anymore. I was consumed with university and work.

I missed the barbecues we used to have at Uncle Mohammad's house on the weekend in his small cosy backyard. The delicious smell of the well-seasoned lamb and chicken kebabs cooking would always bring his next-door neighbours out of their home and they would say hello and chat over the fence. That was Mum's cue to jump to her feet and fill a plate or two with cooked meat skewers wrapped in Arabic bread to keep them warm, cheese-filled *sambousek*, along with some tabouli salad and dips. Hummus, babaganoush and garlic mayonnaise, a perfect accompaniment to the meat. She would ask my brother and cousin to rush the plates over to the neighbours.

Those moments reminded me of the Saudi Arabian weddings in that desert park and how back then often someone would knock on our door and deliver a foil-wrapped parcel full of food then leave without waiting for a thank you. This tradition of sharing food with anyone who can smell it is something my family continued in Australia.

Uncle Mohammad had planted his garden with fruits and herbs that reminded him of home. He had thick bushes of basil, parsley and mint along with a lemon tree and orange, fig and olive trees bunched together in the small garden. But one plant always looked strange to me. It was a travelling vine that didn't look like a fruitful tree, it was stringy and avalanched over his back wooden fence. In summer it would be full of dark green leaves that hid small, perfectly round balls hanging on every vine. It had a name that my mother was embarrassed to say . . . it was a passionfruit. When the fruit was ripe Uncle Mohammad would pick them and slice them open, revealing hundreds of small black seeds covered with orangey-yellow flesh, they looked like little eyes. Each of us would take a half and scoop it out with a spoon, the sweetness and sour bite would make us shake our heads. 'Crunch the seeds,' Uncle Mohammad would say, and with a quick swallow it went down well. I loved it and we all would reach out for another half.

Moments like these seemed rare that year. My life was full of responsibilities and they would get bigger every time Dad would leave. I remember him calling me out to the car one sunny morning and he said he needed to show me how to check the oil in the car and how to change the tyre just in case we got a flat while he was away. As we got older he took the time to prepare us for the things he usually did for our family without us even noticing. That's one of life's ironies, the way we can be in the comfort of a family unit and be to some extent oblivious to how much each member does, but when they leave or pass away we find out how big a gap they leave behind. Changing the oil in the car was something I never even thought about, until then it was just always done for me. Dad would make sure the cars Mum and we girls were driving were running right. He did it without being asked.

I love my father, Hatem, very much. The fact he wasn't always around was something I resented as a teenager. I wanted him there just in case – his mere presence would have been enough. Dad would always call and be up to date with how everything was going while he was gone, but it just wasn't the same as him being there. The hardship of not finding work here in Australia that he would be respected in and could fulfil all his dreams and ours was a harsh reality that left him having to travel between two worlds. Even when things were getting worse in Saudi Arabia economically, I remember Dad still travelling to renew his visa without a promise of work waiting for him. He would stay at his parents' home in Jeddah for months at a time; I guess he missed them. His displacement left him a man of many worlds.

The Year of El Magic

With my father absent so often, I found myself looking for a father figure in my life, someone who would help me make decisions that were important and tell me if this job was better than the other or that subject was more important than this one. I had my three uncles to talk to and they gave me advice and support to my mother but I also sought the wisdom of someone who wasn't a blood relative.

My teacher and mentor Peter Skrzynecki would lend an ear when I came to him with a problem with my work; he would do the same for all his students. He helped each one as much as he could and his sense of encouragement to migrant students was deep and profound. Peter and his family were migrants too, he understood the difficulties of fitting in and he would later say to me something that shattered my cover . . . the cover I'd developed to hide my grammar and spelling problems.

I went to his office and he told me how my essay was written well and had great ideas, but what he said next embarrassed me and liberated me at the same time. 'Don't stick to using words you only know how to spell! You speak so well, you must write the same. Make the dictionary your friend and you will be better than most students in the class because you have a skill most of them don't, you can feel and understand the work.' I was devastated. I thought I was doing a great job at hiding my weakness, but I was wrong. He saw right through me and at that same moment I felt free because I didn't have to pretend anymore.

I walked out of his office and saw life with a different eye, a huge pressure was lifted off my shoulders and from that moment on I thought this is me. I'm not perfect, I'm not always right, but I didn't have to be. *No one* is perfect and I didn't have to struggle to pretend I was or struggle to fit in. I was who I was.

This realisation was so liberating and I will always thank Peter for his guidance.

I was enjoying my studies and, although there were many offers, I'd managed to keep away from any romantic entanglements. There were a few guys at university who were keen and invited me out for a date, but I always said no. They were nice and I was happy to be friends but I was in no place to get to know anyone romantically. I was too busy finding me. I am a big believer in fate and love at first sight, but for me that was much more than some lusting, physical attraction. I believed it meant having a connection, an instant feeling that you have known that person for years despite only just meeting. Do you know that scene in the movie *Sleepless in Seattle* when Tom Hanks talks about his wife? How he describes the moment he knew she was the one and how it was . . . magic. That is what I was looking for.

My idea of love is one that is consuming and inconvenient, butterflies in your stomach every time you think of them, a can't-live-without-you kind of love that makes you forget how you ever lived before them. A-sweep-me-off-my-feet and be-with-you-anywhere kind of love. A love where growing old together is something to look forward to.

It was just a normal day. A university friend had asked me to go with her when she interviewed an upcoming Sydney footballer who happened to be Muslim. He was a player for the Canterbury-Bankstown Bulldogs Rugby League team and was thought to have the potential to be a future star of the game. My friend wasn't Muslim and needed someone to help explain to her any religious

The Year of El Magic

and cultural references he might make. I wasn't keen. I had my opinion about footballers; but she was persuasive and reluctantly I said yes. After all, I just had to listen and help her later, I didn't have to do much myself.

She booked the interview for Thursday, 12 June 1997. It was a beautiful winter morning, cold but sunny and crisp and I wasn't thinking about much at all as I drove to uni. Just as I parked, my phone rang. It was my friend saying she was really sick, but she couldn't reschedule the interview – she begged me to do it for her. My answer was an emphatic 'no!' The idea of going to a football club full of men, on my own, was not a comfortable one for me. I knew my parents wouldn't approve, in fact they would have been horrified.

She begged me and I still refused until she began to cry. I crumbled and said yes, but I also told her I didn't know much about football and football players, but the image I had of athletes in general was not good. I don't quite know where my opinion came from, but that day I was expecting this Hazem El Masri to be rude and womanising. I wasn't going to let him or anyone else treat me with disrespect.

I got in the car and drove off as though something was guiding me there. I had never been to Belmore before and, being from Liverpool, it was a place I was unfamiliar with; but it took me only fifteen minutes to get there. The roads were nearly empty and all the traffic lights were green. Belmore Oval is nestled among houses and shops and you can easily miss it if you don't know it's there. As I drove up the narrow driveway to the car park, houses lined the right side and their backyard gates opened on to the narrow road. Before I knew it I was parking my car at Belmore sports ground. I watched a group of men run past me outside the stadium and I didn't recognise any of them, although I'd seen the

Bulldogs play on TV during Friday night football. I sometimes watched half-heartedly just to connect with my brothers.

I didn't know much about football, its rules or the players, just that the Bulldogs were popular among people at university. As soon as I got to the gate I saw some pictures of Bulldogs and a sign pointed to the Terry Lamb stand. As I walked around to the field, the smell of freshly mown grass was in the air. I took a deep breath. It was such a peaceful spot, I wanted to lie down on the grass and watch the clouds all day. That thought was broken when a passing train drowned out the serenity. What an awful backdrop to an oval that was so beautiful, but the train noise wouldn't even be noticed once the stands were full of thousands of fans cheering for the Bulldogs.

I did as my friend told me and sat and waited in the stand for the team to come out and train, but no one did. I hated being there. Half an hour passed and a man on a lawnmower trimming that flawless grass came up to me and said, 'Hi! Are you waiting for someone?'

I told him I had an interview with someone called Hazem El Masri. He offered to show me to the office so they could let him know I was there. So I went into the office and sat and waited. I looked up as a man walked in and it was Terry Lamb talking to the receptionist. I said hello because I recognised him.

I was getting nervous waiting and finally one of the club's managers, a softly spoken man in his sixties, came up to me and said, 'Hi, love, my name is Allan Nelson. Hazem's just finishing up. Would you like to come down to the tunnel and I will arrange for Hazem to meet us there when he is done?' I was hesitant but he assured me we would stay out of the team dressing area and he took me for a tour. We ended up at the mouth of the Belmore tunnel looking out onto the field and the whole time he kept on about how much he liked Hazem and how he thought he was so talented. I nodded in respect, but wasn't completely paying attention. We were standing in the sun waiting for this Hazem guy and I started to get annoyed that he was taking his time.

The team manager, Fred, came and joined us and he started asking me questions like, 'So . . . you're from Hazem's background, hey?' and 'Are you Muslim, too?' I replied that I was and then he said, 'So, we could be looking at the next Mrs El Masri!' I turned and gave him the dirtiest look possible and said icily, 'I don't think so!' He was very red-faced and apologised when he realised he had offended me but I was too shocked to respond. At just that moment Hazem turned up.

I was standing in the sun and the tunnel was dark, so all I could see was the shadow of a person walking towards us. He could see me but I couldn't see him. As he reached the end of the tunnel his body came into the light and the sun hit his face. Our eyes met for the first time . . . and I almost gasped. I felt as though I had known this man for a hundred years even though he hadn't said a word to me yet. His beautiful brown eyes held a slight reluctance to look me in the eye, that shyness caught my attention. Could it be out of respect?

I introduced myself, 'Hi, my name is Arwa. I'm from the University of Western Sydney and I just have a few questions for you.' I nodded a greeting and his eyes met mine for a lingering moment, which sent a shiver down my body and that feeling of butterflies in my stomach. I managed to hide how I was feeling and maintain my composure, but inside my thoughts were swirling – *Why do I feel this way? What is this feeling that has consumed me?*

Hazem spoke with a voice that I swear I must have heard in a past life, it was so familiar and comforting. He led the way towards the grandstand so we could sit, but he took one look at the filthy seats and before I could say anything he used the edge of his singlet to wipe down my chair before saying, 'Take a seat.' I couldn't believe it. How could this young man, *a footballer*, be so decent and respectful of me and make me feel like I did? So much more decent than some of those young men I had met with degrees and well-paid jobs? In my mind, as a footballer he was supposed to be rude and womanising, but he was obviously the absolute opposite.

The beer-drinking culture and party-hard attitudes of footballers was something everyone talked about so I couldn't help wondering if he was putting on an act or if he really was different. But I knew deep down that he was genuine. It was the strangest thing, I maintained my composure and remained critical even though there was a voice in my head telling me he was the one. What an unlikely person for me to feel this way towards: an athlete, a rugby league footballer, and Lebanese-born not Palestinian. He didn't fit the mould of a man my parents would hope for me; he was not a doctor and didn't have a degree. This couldn't be! I would later wonder where this image of the 'right' person came from and I realised it was based on my father. In my mind the 'one' had to live up to his standard.

I can't explain how I felt about Hazem at that first meeting other than to say that it was not in my control. Something had brought me there that day, something powerful. We sat a seat apart and I said, 'This shouldn't take long, I just have a few questions for you about what it is like to be the first professional Muslim rugby league player.' He looked at the ground thoughtfully as he carefully answered all my questions. I was a bit flustered because I'd left my notepad in the car and I didn't feel I could race back and get it. I had to remember all his answers.

The Year of El Magic

We began to chat and he told me he had just returned from Mecca a few months before. He'd gone with some friends to perform the out-of-Hajj season pilgrimage *Umrah*. My mind started questioning why this young footballer, at the beginning of his career and with all the lifestyle distractions associated with being an up-and-coming first-grade footballer, would be going to Mecca? Was he really disinterested in the girls, the money and everything in between? I could already see that he was focused and determined to play football and it seemed the hype didn't distract him.

A ten-minute interview turned into a forty-minute chat that went very quickly. We talked about both our experiences coming to Australia and I didn't want to leave. But finally I had to say, 'It was nice talking with you and I wish you all the best.'

I stood and started to walk away, but I didn't know the way out. He said, 'Can you wait and I will walk you to your car?' He ran back down the tunnel and I could feel my heart beating waiting for him to return; it was the longest five minutes. I didn't hint at how I was feeling so I stayed composed. When he came back we started to walk out to the car park and he nervously said, 'Just in case you need more details for your article, do you mind if I give you my number?'

I couldn't help myself; that feisty proud woman in me came out and I asked him if he gave his number to everyone who interviewed him. He replied, 'No. Only the ones who forget to bring a notebook!' We both smiled as he passed me his number. I got in my car and he watched me drive off.

I couldn't stop thinking about Hazem that whole night. I was so overwhelmed. This guy had made more of an impression on me than anyone I had ever known. The thought of him consumed me and I tried to ignore it, but then putting the interview together over the next few days I realised I needed to ask just one more question, or so I told myself. I called his mobile and left a message on voicemail. I couldn't have been happier when he called me back instantly. I asked the question, thanked him again for his answer and then we chatted a little bit. Hazem said, 'Maybe I will see you around the uni campus gym, I train there sometimes since I don't live very far away.' I told him I trained there sometimes too, so maybe I would see him. As soon as I hung up I called Abeer and told her I had met the most amazing guy; decent, respectful and with the warmest brown eyes that drew me in the first time I saw him.

The first thing Abeer said was, 'What is it about him you liked?' I told her, then I stopped myself. I realised I'd been guilty of something I always hated. Because he was a footballer I had stereotyped Hazem before I'd even met him as fitting the mould of footballers I'd read about in the papers. I'd done something to him I never wanted done to me and hated seeing being done to others. How paradoxical that we can disapprove of prejudice directed at us, yet have no hesitation in directing our own prejudice at someone else. Some call it the nature of the beast, but I call it double standards and hypocrisy. I was guilty! Without preaching about his good nature, meeting Hazem showed me my prejudice. Footballers, like any other occupation, are all individuals and are responsible for their own behaviour and should not be lumped together under a preconceived stereotype because of the actions of a minority in that occupation. Nationality, skin colour, race, job, height or anything else is not a reason for bad behaviour, they are tools of prejudice. People blame these identifying factors rather than an individual because it makes us feel better that we are able to pinpoint the problem and keep away from it. I was

The Year of El Magic

ashamed that I had done just that in assuming Hazem El Masri was one of a pack. He was anything but!

Hazem and I began a friendship that would be built on mutual respect. He was always polite and considerate in every way, his sense of humour was different to mine, but he made me laugh often and I was happy when he was around. His life experiences were very different from mine and meeting him opened my eyes to a struggle that was common among war refugees. His parents, Khaled and Amal, didn't speak any English when they arrived in Australia. The war in Lebanon had prevented Hazem from attending regular schooling so his education had been severely disrupted; that experience affected his appetite for learning. Going to school for him and his family and friends meant a fast run down the main street in Tripoli while trying to avoid bombs flying above their heads. The echoes of gunfire and the smell of gunpowder would regularly fill the air as terrified children were comforted by a frantic parent telling them that everything was going to be okay. Whatever happened to the notion of smiling kids holding hands and waving goodbye to mum as they head out to meet their friends on a sunny Monday morning? It was a world away from my school days and it was no wonder Hazem's motivation and willingness to learn was hindered by constant fear and instability.

He directed his attention to his natural-born talent: a love for sport, and especially soccer. He excelled at anything physical and when he was kicking the ball he escaped the horrible reality of the war that surrounded him, even if it was only for a few hours. He never knew why things were the way they were but he knew it was not how things should be. Khaled, Hazem's father, was not going to let his kids grow up in these circumstances, so he began to look for a new home for his family that was safe and far away from the war in Lebanon. Yet again a man looking for a better life for his children found the answer in Australia.

I would see Hazem often in the uni gym and we would end up sitting outside on the lawn talking for hours. We shared our life stories and the experiences that only another migrant would understand. We both had experienced feelings of being different and of wanting so badly to belong. We both admitted to having that place where our hearts yearned to visit – we missed it. For us both, our lives began in one place and ended up in another, but how had we come together? Was it because our hearts were torn between two places? Was it our displacement that brought us together or something beyond that? Did we see our troubles in each other's eyes, or was it our shared desire to belong? Whatever it was, Australia brought us together. It made me think about my parents and the way my new home was changing the expectations I had for the 'other' who would share my life.

I had wondered many times how my parents came to be together. They'd both been forced to leave their country and had met in Saudi Arabia. Had they been looking for something in each other that only the other knew was there? A sense of being lost and finding some of yourself in someone else? Was it true love, far from any reasonable or logical equation? Was there a connection or a deeply rooted magnetism due to their similar situation?

Now, with Hazem in my life, I needed to know what my mother had seen in my father, why he had become the man who would share her life. Or were they together because they were both Palestinian? And if that was the case, was that enough for two people to be linked to each other for life? I had to ask and my mother told me when I asked her to define her relationship with my father that it was simple – 'It was someone Palestinian or nothing else.' It wasn't a decision based on prejudice, but by her displacement. With all the unrest in Palestine the casualties were decades long and things looked grim. She saw it as her responsibility to continue the bloodline to ensure that Palestinians didn't just disappear.

My mother didn't deny that she loved my father and was attracted to him, but for her it was Palestinian first and everything else second. It was the same for Dad, he would have only married a Palestinian woman. Here I was at a crossroads and I had to make a choice: should I do as my parents had done and assume a responsibility to Palestine or follow my heart?

I grew fonder of Hazem by the day and each time I was with him I realised more and more how wrong my prejudices about him had been. He was a complete gentleman and had been raised by a mother who showed him how to treat a woman with respect, just as she had been treated by his father. We never spoke about how we felt about one another, but I could tell he enjoyed my company as much as I did his. He never invaded my personal space or made me feel uncomfortable. Whenever we were together it was never long enough. But I didn't know what would become of our friendship, or whether I was brave enough to be with someone who my parents would judge because he was a football player. And was I imagining something more than friendship was there anyway? I can see now I cared too much about what people thought and was trying to second-guess my parents' expectations of me. I was torn and didn't think I could stand up and fight for Hazem, especially when I didn't even know if he felt the same way.

Then something happened that forced me to decide what was truly important to me. It would shake our connection to its core and showed me that true love demands courage. I was caught between what I thought I should do and how I wanted to live my life when an old family friend spoke to my father to propose that their son ask for my hand in marriage. It was a traditional marriage proposal, not an arranged one; my parents would never stand for that as Islam teaches that a woman's consent to marriage is paramount and that if she is pressured the marriage can be declared void.

I saw Hazem the next day and told him. His reaction would tell me everything I needed to know. He was pale faced and quiet for a long time as I told him the news of my impending engagement, then he said, 'Well, if you're happy then congratulations.' The truth was, I wasn't happy. The young man who proposed was a lovely person, I knew him and his family well. He was Palestinian and a pharmacist with a good family, all the boxes were ticked except for one – he wasn't Hazem.

I wanted Hazem to say '*No! Don't do it! I love you and want to be with you, say no and we can be together forever,*' but he didn't. My heart was bleeding, but I showed him nothing. I'd obviously been wrong, he just saw me as a friend who was now marrying someone else and he was happy for me.

The next month would teach me a valuable lesson. I had made a horrible mistake and I was now engaged to someone who fitted the mould of what others expected of the man I would marry. I was depressed and frightened at what a loveless marriage would do to me. My need for my parents' approval could have destroyed any chance I had with someone I felt so strongly about. I couldn't be with someone while I was constantly thinking of someone else, it wasn't fair to anyone. I remember praying to Allah and asking him for guidance. I didn't know what to do and I felt Allah's guidance; all my fears withered away and my heart was calm and without fear. I knew what I had to do.

The next morning I went to the only man who would understand and help me, my father. That conversation with my dad was so

The Year of El Magic

awkward. I couldn't look him in the eye and the one time I did he looked so concerned. But he was to show me a love that superseded any embarrassment this situation would bring to him personally. He asked me why I didn't tell him earlier that I had no attraction to this young man. I wasn't ready to tell him yet – that he just wasn't Hazem. I gave my father the ring I had been given.

My father hugged me and said, 'I will call them and you don't need to worry about a thing.' Our engagement was to have been announced at a big party, people were invited and pictures were taken of us, so we weren't going to be able to keep this situation a private affair. People would talk and I felt bad for the man I had agreed to marry. I was in my room crying and my grandmother Hindiya came in and said to me, 'Better now than later.' She knew of my friendship with Hazem and she whispered in my ear as she kissed me, 'You did the right thing . . . follow your heart, my dear.'

For the entire month while all this was going on I didn't contact Hazem, nor he me. I was on my summer holidays from university and I hadn't seen him; it was the longest time of uncertainty. Was he going to be happy at the news? Was I even going to see him again? The holidays were soon over and I went back to university hopeful. I went to the gym a few times to see if he was there but he never was. Then finally one day I spotted him. He came up to me and said hello. He looked happy and sad at the same time, but I still wasn't sure how he felt. We sat outside on the grass and talked and then he nervously asked me, 'How's your fiancé?' I told him that it was over and that he hadn't been the right guy for me.

It would be a few months before Hazem told me how much that ordeal had hurt him. He told me how he felt something the day we first met and that he was sure I'd felt it too, so he couldn't understand what had happened. And now I was feeling afraid and was sailing uncharted territory. It was an act of bravery and courage for me to stand up and choose differently to what my mother had. I didn't know I was capable of such bravery until I made the mistake of following expectations. My heart revealed to me that I was indeed a woman with courage, willing to stand alone for the right reasons.

Finally I heard what I was waiting to hear since the day I met him. 'I knew you were the one, too.' The team manager was right, I was going to be Mrs El Masri, something that had offended me then now honoured me. A few weeks later Hazem would buy a ring and wait for the right moment and, in the style of a true romantic novel, he got down on one knee and asked, 'Will you marry me?' Of course the answer was yes.

But that wasn't the end of it. Hazem then had to make his proposal to my father. His mother wasted no time in making sure that happened and the phone rang while I was at home the next day and I could hear my mother saying, 'We will see you then, Mrs El Masri.' My father asked me who this fellow was and I told him all about Hazem. I saw deep concern in my father's eyes as soon as he heard he was a football player, the same concerns I had felt initially. He said to me, 'You don't know what that lifestyle is like. What if his job is something you can't deal with? The life of a sportsman is one that is busy, unstable and filled with distractions, are you ready to deal with all that?'

I could tell Dad was worried about Hazem's consciousness of Islam and was concerned whether I had thought of all the things he would be exposed to as a result of his job. Dad was doing exactly what I had done, defining Hazem's conduct as improper without any proof or knowledge of him. It was time to use that diplomacy I was gifted with.

It was my job to properly introduce Dad to rugby league. We watched the Bulldogs play on Friday night that week and I pointed Hazem out to my parents. I remember Dad asking me, 'Why do they have to bring each other down to the ground? Why isn't it enough to just hold them for a few seconds?' and 'Why is that guy not in front of the one passing the ball? And why are they passing the ball backwards?' I could tell he didn't like the game, perhaps because he didn't understand it or thought it was very rough. But in time he would grow to love it and he'd be asking me when the next match was and who was leading the competition. Gradually, Dad would take a special interest in Hazem's football career as he saw him make something of it that was far beyond the athletic achievements he was praised for. Both my parents regard Hazem very highly and think the world of him, even though his life is so different from theirs.

The day Hazem and his parents came over to meet my parents, I was so concerned Dad wasn't going to like him. When they walked in my heart was pounding and I remember Hazem looked nervously handsome. We all sat down and everyone began to chat. Hazem hardly said a word to Dad, but Dad was watching him carefully. I sat on the seat next to Hazem and his mother. The conversations seemed to be going well so my dad decided to tell an embarrassing story about when we were in the United States. I have had to hear this story for many years and as soon as my father finishes telling it he laughs uncontrollably.

Apparently, when I was a three-year-old in Arizona, my sisters and I were playing with some of our American friends in the front yard and one of them asked us all, 'Where are you from?' Each child said where they came from in America, and when it was my sisters' turn they both said they were from Palestine. When it was my turn I copied our friend Rebecca and said, 'I'm from California!' I can't tell you why Dad loves that story so much, but I think it's because it displays the innocence of a child and how belonging is an instinctive feeling that gets harder to find as you get older and your world expands. Dad asked Hazem a few tough questions and I could tell he was impressed with Hazem's responses.

When it came time to say goodbye, my father closed the door and I stood by him waiting to hear what he thought of the man I wanted to marry. Dad turned to me and said something I never thought he would. 'I don't think you'll find a better man than Hazem, the respect he showed his parents and me and your mum tonight is proof that he has been raised well and deserves to be with you.' I was over the moon. I was so happy, all my concerns that this would never work were put to rest. The two most important men in my life liked each other and were going to get along just fine.

Chicken kebabs

Ingredients

    2kg skinless chicken thigh fillets
    2 tsp salt
    1 tsp ground pimento
    1 tsp ground cinnamon
    ½ tsp ground black pepper
    2 tsp sweet paprika
    ¼ tsp dried chilli flakes (optional)
    6 garlic cloves, crushed
    Zest and juice 1 lemon
    ½ cup extra virgin olive oil

Method

Trim the chicken and cut each piece into quarters. In a deep bowl add all the other ingredients and mix well. Add the chicken and set aside for an hour in the fridge for the flavours to absorb, alternatively you can use it right away.

Skewer the pieces, not over-filling each skewer, and cook on a hot barbecue of charcoal or gas flame. Enjoy with Arab bread, garlic dip and fresh tabouli salad.

Note: you can leave the chicken fillets whole if you wish, you can also use chicken breast fillets for the kebabs.

Serves 6 to 8 people.

Lamb kebabs

Ingredients

- 1 tbs salt
- 3 tsp ground pimento
- 1 tsp cinnamon
- 1 tsp ground black pepper
- 2kg of trimmed lamb fillets cut into small to medium sized pieces
- ¼ cup extra virgin olive oil
- 6 garlic cloves, crushed
- 2 tbs fresh rosemary leaves, chopped finely
- Zest of 1 lemon

Method

In a large bowl add the dry spices and mix them together. Add the lamb and rub the spices into the meat using your hands. In a separate bowl mix together the olive oil, garlic, rosemary and lemon zest. Add them to the meat and rub them in well. Set aside for an hour or more for best taste. Skewer the lamb and cook it on a barbecue. Enjoy with Arab bread, babaganoush and Spanish onion salad.

Serves 6 to 8 people.

Spanish onion salad

Finely slice 2 Spanish red onions and place in a bowl. Roughly chop a small bunch of flat-leaf parsley and add to onion. Add a teaspoon of sumac and a small pinch of salt and mix well. Enjoy with lamb kebabs.

Arwa's cheese and herb sambousek

Ingredients

- 1 cup grated haloumi cheese
- 1 cup grated Akawi cheese
- 1 cup Danish feta in small pieces
- 1 cup ricotta cheese
- ½ cup grated tasty cheese
- ½ cup grated mozzarella
- 1 tbs Nigella seeds
- 1 tbs dried mint leaves
- ½ cup chopped flat-leaf parsley
- ½ cup chopped spinach leaves
- ¼ cup fresh oregano leaves
- Zest of 1 lemon
- 1 tsp ground black pepper
- 1 egg, beaten
- 6 sheets of puff pastry

Method

Combine all the cheeses in a large bowl, mixing gently. Add the rest of the ingredients, except the pastry, and mix well being careful not to mash the mix. Cut the pastry into quarters and fill with 2 tablespoons of the mix. Seal to form a triangle and pinch the edges tightly. Place on a slightly greased baking tray and make a small cut in the top of the pastry to let out the steam. Bake in a hot oven (200°C) till golden brown. You may need more pastry depending on how much you fill each triangle.

Makes 16 to 20 cheese triangles.

Chapter Nine
A Formal Engagement

I was the youngest girl in our family and yet I was the first to become engaged, though Maha and Reem weren't far behind. Maha had received many proposals the traditional way: these men would come and introduce their family to my parents and after a visit or two Maha would tell Dad she wasn't interested and he would apologise and tell them it wasn't going to happen. The traditional marriage proposal is a difficult one to explain, it seems as though the woman is being paraded for the approval of the male suitor, but the fact is exactly the opposite; he is presenting himself to her and expressing his interest. But the woman has the final say as to whether she likes what she sees or not. If a man doesn't express interest he will never know what a woman ever thought of him. In this case, the woman is protected from embarrassment, but the man needs to be brave and present himself for a knockback.

This type of marriage proposal is sometimes misused by some cultures in the Middle East and around the world. The young woman is paraded in a fashion that isn't dignified and without being allowed to talk to the male suitor, she is then asked by her parents what she thinks of him from a first glance. I remember

Maha telling me about one of her school friends, Layla, in Saudi Arabia who got married while she was still finishing school; they were both in Year Twelve. Layla seemed unhappy when she invited Maha to her engagement party. Maha was curious and worried why something that is supposed to be a happy occasion was making her friend miserable. Layla told Maha how she was only allowed to see the man once and when her father asked her for an answer she said, 'I want to see him again and talk to him.' Her father was furious and slapped her in a rage. She went to her room and her mother told her, 'He is a good boy, from a good family, what else do you want to know? Just say yes and you can get to know him after you are married, just like I did.'

From that moment Maha's mind was made up, she wasn't going to be with just anyone. Islam encourages the interaction of young men and women wanting to get married, but only in a fashion that respects Islamic guidelines. So getting to know each other and talking on many occasions, even going out and visiting each other's homes, is acceptable, so long as there's a parent present who respects their privacy. These traditions are not restricted to Islam, they are common among other cultures such as the Italian and Greek.

The many suitors who had made themselves known to Maha in Australia were all Arabs, and after a few had come and gone I began to feel Maha was looking for something else. Maha is a beautiful woman, she has fair hair and bright blue eyes and so, like me, she was never picked as being Arab. She could be critical of certain traditions in our culture that have nothing to do with Islam. She questioned things that made no sense, was it religious or cultural? She was proud of her culture but not willing to bow to culture when it contradicted religion. She had become certain after a few years she could never be with that kind of

A Formal Engagement

Arab man. Even though she was the eldest she wasn't worried if she married last. She wasn't going to be with just anyone, it had to be someone who was her soul mate. I guess Maha and I saw love the same way, love was worth breaking the rules for. Islam doesn't differentiate between races in any way and when it comes to marriage it is no different.

Maha married a man called John. An Anglo-Australian, I respect him very much: he was raised a Christian and converted to Islam. His reasons weren't only marriage but as he got to know Islam he found that the life he lives is not far from the way Maha did and he found Islam a comfortable fit. Like Hazem, he was another gentleman. John was raised by a Christian mother who taught him how to respect a woman, which means it's not a cultural or racial thing but a human one that binds and attracts us to what is right and honourable in each other.

I was now at a new point in my life, marrying a person who was different to me, or so I thought. Lebanon and Palestine are neighbours, one line separates us from each other. The lines that separate us, as do the rest of the borders in the Middle East, were laid down by the British and French who colonised these parts of the Arab world. People had travelled without borders for centuries, passing through countries and announcing their arrival with only a raised palm and a nod of the head, saying '*assalamu alaikum*', peace be upon you. That's all it took. Now for any Arab to travel between the countries of the Middle East, even if it is to a country right on its border you need a visa – often something Westerners don't need when travelling to the same places. Why was this? The Middle Eastern history I learned of as a child in

Saudi Arabia told of times that made me feel safe and proud to be an Arab, a dignified existence and one without division, but this is only in the history books as the reality of the Middle East today is nothing like what it had been.

My parents always taught my siblings and me to be proud of our nationality; to announce that I am of Palestinian heritage is something that always makes me proud. Although my passport now declares me Australian, that feeling of belonging here was something that grew with time, it wasn't an overnight transition. And before that happened I often wondered, am I supposed to forget and forfeit all of me to be accepted, and how much of me was Australia willing to allow? If I said that I was Palestinian before I became an Australian citizen would people find that strange? I am both and for a while I was between nationalities, unique and lost to some extent, not entirely like one or the other but a blend producing a new identity that takes the best of both worlds. All these thoughts were part of my initial acceptance of that traditional marriage proposal and my fear in following my heart. And yet, once I overcame this fear it was never a problem. And now, Hazem's and my children know that their dad is Lebanese–Australian and their mum is Palestinian–Australian, and that they are Aussies with migrant parents. I am sure they won't have the complications of the heart that I had, but I wish it had been easier for others like me.

How do we explain this new subculture, a blend of two things? There are many who question whether multiculturalism really works or whether it is a myth. Are we all just yearning to go back to where we came from if we had a chance? The mass migrations in the world that have occurred as a result of wars have left so many people homeless; these people who migrated abroad in most cases yearn to go back at some time or other, even if it is

A Formal Engagement

just for a long visit. But in Hazem I had found my home and it was thanks to my new country that I'd found my soul mate.

Traditionally an engagement party is held at the bride's home and Hazem's and mine was no different. My parents' new home was the perfect place for the ceremony and party. The Islamic engagement party is a little different to the Australian equivalent as there is an imam, or leader in prayer, who performs some traditional parts of what would be considered an Australian marriage ceremony. In effect, the man and the woman are married under Islamic law after this ceremony but until the formal wedding process and marriage certificate is signed they should not live together as husband and wife. It is a very traditional and quite conservative process that Hazem and I were happy to follow in respect to our parents and traditional custom.

I had my dress handmade by a friend, who was a talented dressmaker. I would have asked Reem but she was too busy. She had received her own marriage proposal, a traditional one. Her fiancé, Akheel, and his family had visited my parents and they were always chatting and getting to know each other. These visits would go on for weeks but I knew they liked each other from the first time they met. The traditional marriage proposal doesn't work for everyone, but in Reem and Akheel's case it did, they truly are a perfect fit.

My mother and I had visited the fabric shops of Cabramatta in Sydney's western suburbs to find the material for my dress. Cabramatta is famous for its fabric stores, among other things. You can walk down the street and see and smell the aroma of the East. A tapestry of Asian cultures fills its streets, with sushi and sugarcane juice sold on the footpath. Greengrocers there sold fruits and vegetables I had never before seen, my mother and I stopped and picked up a familiar-looking fruit, it was a custard apple, but it was the only one we recognised. The inside of a custard apple is like individual black gemstones coated with sweet and soft white flesh that comes away with the slightest touch. I love this fruit, so humble and unique; we used to eat it regularly in Saudi Arabia and continued to do so when in Sydney. Walking through the shops Mum and I could see the Buddha statues at nearly every store and beneath the statue there would be a plate filled with fruit as an offering and you can guarantee a custard apple was among them.

As I stopped to buy some custard apples I spotted a small prickly ball that looked like a rock. The woman selling them said to me, 'Taste one', but I didn't know how. Seeing my confusion she began to peel one, revealing a grape-like fruit. It was a lychee. The Asian woman put it in her mouth and after a few chews spat out a seed and said to us again, 'Try it!' Mum and I both did, and it was delicious. We bought a kilo and took them home to share with the rest of the family. We were proud to have discovered a new native Asian fruit that is now grown in Australia.

With all the distractions of the Asian food market I hadn't forgotten what I'd come for. I was on a mission to find the right coloured fabric for my sleeveless dress. I wanted it to be satin with a hint of shine and I needed a matching chiffon to cover my shoulders when the imam performed the Islamic marriage ceremony and asked me if I would take Hazem for my husband. We looked at all the shops and at last I found it, a sage-green fabric that reminded me of the dill leaves that Hindiya loved so much. We asked the man to cut us six metres and then we were off home. When we got there Hindiya was waiting to see my choice of fabric. When I took it out of the bag she smiled and said, 'It's the same colour as a dress I used to have when I was your age.' Even taste can be hereditary. My dressmaker came to

A Formal Engagement

my home for all the fittings and Hindiya and Mum were always there to offer advice on how the dress should fit; they were both talented seamstresses. With all their advice and the dressmaker's skill the dress turned out to be perfect.

The day of my official engagement to Hazem was filled with preparations by both families. Hazem's parents were in charge of the food and my family in preparing the venue. Amal had ordered two huge trays of *kunafa* to serve the seventy guests. *Kunafa* is a traditional sweet popular in the Middle East, especially at engagements, weddings and sometimes funerals; the Lebanese *kunafa* is made with a thin layer of carefully prepared fine semolina base filled with the traditional Arab cream, *ashta*, or sweet cheese, and topped with another layer of semolina baked to perfection, drizzled with cold sugar syrup, decorated with more *ashta* and sprinkled with a generous heap of crushed pistachio nuts. There are many different variations across the Middle East. Palestinians make it with stringy dough filled with sweet cheese, but that night we diplomatically agreed on having the Lebanese version.

I was so happy and nervous that day. I had hair and beautician appointments to get to, along with my makeup, which Maha helped me do. As night began to fall the guests started to arrive. Traditionally the engagement is for close family and friends who witness the occasion, so of course my dear friend Abeer was there. I watched as Hazem arrived with his family, peeking out from behind a curtain my mother had hung to separate the kitchen from the rest of the house so none of the men would wander into the women's room. He looked so handsome dressed in a sharp black suit. The lounge room was full and the imam began the Islamic marriage ceremony, Hazem sitting to his right and my father sitting to his left. The Islamic marriage ceremony states the rights and obligations of each spouse along with the amount of dowry that is given to the bride. The imam reads passages from the Quran that are relevant to the marriage and he blesses the union.

While Hazem was sitting beside the imam I was standing outside the room with my sage-green chiffon covering my hair and bare shoulders. I was invited to go in but I was too nervous to enter a room full of seventy or so guests, so I stayed outside the door where I could see Hazem and he could see me. When it was time for the imam to ask me if I accepted Hazem for a husband, he walked up to me as I was joined by both Hazem's parents and mine. The imam looked at me and said, 'Do you, Arwa, take Hazem as your husband?' He needed to see my face to determine whether I was being pressured into the marriage or not and he had the right to refuse the marriage if he saw this was the case. Islam requires unpressured and uncoerced acceptance from the bride otherwise the marriage can be declared void. He asked me the same question three times and with my final answer he jokingly said, 'Are you sure? Because I hear he is a very busy man.' We laughed and we both signed the marriage certificate and just like that we were married in Islamic law. This meant we were able to go out together without a chaperone. This stage of marriage doesn't forbid the consummation of the marriage, but it is preferred to wait until the official ceremony has been celebrated with family and friends. But there are other social reasons too.

A close friend of mine was in that situation; she was engaged to a man she loved and was married to him in Islamic law but the actual wedding was four months away. They did what people in love do and consummated the marriage before the wedding. She became pregnant and had to tell her mother, who then rushed the wedding forward. The ceremony was filled with curious eyes and after eight months she gave birth to her first son. People's nosy suspicions were confirmed, and even though they didn't do anything forbidden in Islam they were still looked at differently by people who knew because they had not shown restraint and respected the complete marriage ritual.

The imam obviously saw the happiness on my face because he declared me and Hazem married. The flow of *kunafa*-filled plates started making their way into the room and Hazem's brothers and mine pitched in to serve the delicious sweet along with Dad's perfectly brewed Turkish coffee. My grandmother Hindiya was so happy for me. I walked over and knelt down beside her and kissed her hands and she smiled and said, 'May Allah bless you and give you a good life.'

Once coffee cups were empty most of the guests left and our private family celebration began with Hazem, me and our families. My mother put together the most beautiful flower arrangements for the occasion, one of them sat on a table between my seat and Hazem's. We stood up and then it was time to exchange rings. Hazem and I had chosen them together. Mine was gold with a classic princess-cut diamond and there was a matching wedding band also studded with diamonds to go alongside it. I loved it, and so did our mothers, who were with us when we were shopping for it. He took my hand and slid the ring on my finger and then I put his modest silver wedding band on his (Islam prohibits men to wear gold jewellery and Hazem was happy to abide) and the exchange was complete. We were now officially a couple.

That night we danced together for the first time. We were both so happy and when I looked at him I felt such a connection. He put his arm around me for the first time and it felt just right and comfortable. As our families clapped to the beat of the Arabic music playing, some even joined in the dance. I wanted that moment to last forever. When it was time to go, Hazem told me to get ready to go on our first date as an engaged couple the next evening. I was so excited and couldn't wait till I saw him again. I knew without a doubt that we had both followed our hearts and I knew that this was the man I was meant to be with.

Dad's Turkish coffee

You will need a traditional coffee pot for this recipe.

Ingredients

    2 cups water, boiled in the coffee pot
    4 tbs sugar (optional)
    4 tbs fine ground Turkish or Arabic coffee
    5 cardamom pods

Method

When the water has come to the boil add the sugar and stir, keeping it on the heat. Add the coffee carefully while stirring gently and then add the cardamom seeds after bruising them with a knife to release their flavour. Boil for 5 minutes then set aside to rest. Pour and enjoy with dates or cake.

Makes 8 espresso-sized servings.

Chapter Ten

Mrs El Masri

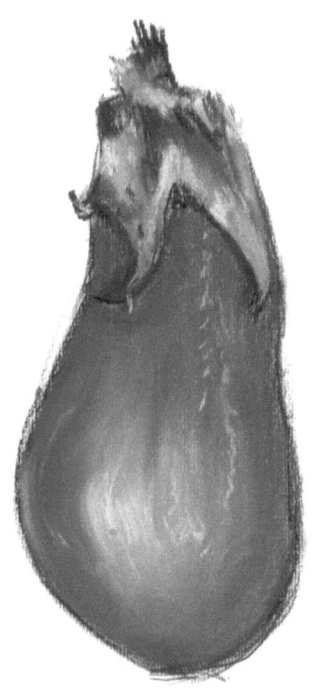

With our engagement now official, Hazem and I were able to go out together without a chaperone. As he'd promised, Hazem came over the next evening to take me out to dinner. I had been excited about it all day and was looking forward to being with him on our own. My father stood at the door as we left and said in a deep fatherly voice, 'Don't be late, be home by eleven.' He was so solemn and I was by comparison almost giddy with happiness. Hazem was the ultimate respectful gentleman: he acknowledged my father and opened the car door for me. We drove off, both happy that we were finally alone.

I knew Hazem had booked dinner for the two of us, but he asked if we could make a quick stop at the Royal Prince Alfred hospital in the city before we went to dinner. I was worried that someone in his family was ill but he told me it was 'Just a friend' so I didn't ask further. When we got to the hospital he parked the car and said, 'I will try not to be long, I promise.' Half an hour later he came back and he looked sad; I asked if the person he visited was okay. It turned out a young boy had been hit by a car and as a result had to have his leg amputated. He was a mad Bulldogs supporter and someone had called Hazem just before he picked me up to ask if he would visit the boy. He was struggling to come to terms with what had happened and needed a boost. Hazem had no hesitation in wanting to cheer the boy up and was happy to take the time to see him.

I was so touched and it reinforced what I already knew, that Hazem was a compassionate man. But it also told me something else about him – that I was never going to have him all to myself. To this day his willingness to do a good thing at all hours without the need for any thanks means his children and I have to share him. That's the man Hazem is and when you hear that kind of story you don't mind being second on his list of priorities. Hazem is seen as a role model in the Australian community and I am extremely proud of that, but I am more proud of the fact that he is a great father and sets a good example for our children every day in everything he does. Hazem will stop the car on a hill, jump out and help an old man pushing his broken-down car in pouring rain. As our kids look on they ask me, 'Who is that man Dad's helping, Mum?' and I would say, 'I don't know, darling, he's just someone who needs a hand.'

Our date that evening was wonderful and the night passed quickly; it would be one of many we would go on before our wedding. After four or so dates Hazem took me to Clovelly Beach, even though it was cold and windy and the sea was in a fury. The natural beauty of the coastline that surrounds Australia always takes my breath away. We sat at the edge of the rocks, looking at the waves crashing down with the ocean spray catching us once or twice. We were both cold so we came closer together. I rested my back on Hazem's chest, facing the sea, and he wrapped his arms around me to keep me warm. I felt so safe and comfortable. It was our first moment alone that we will always remember.

Hazem and I were engaged for just over a year and during those months we focused on getting our home ready for our married life. We both would have liked to have been married sooner, but with Dad's travels and Hazem's football commitments we had to be patient. Hazem had bought his first home when we became engaged and, being the son of a carpenter, he was more than ready to fix it up himself. He takes pride in doing something and does it well. For our new home he painted, put in new lighting, ripped up old carpet and had the floorboards polished. I appreciate that about him very much, he is an invaluable handyman around the house.

The house had a pool and a garden bed ready for our own herb and vegetable patch, and it had an old woodstove fireplace that reminded me of the one that was in the house we lived in in Grafton. Mum used to warm the Arab bread on top while the teapot bubbled beside it. The smell of fresh baked bread would fill the house and always made me feel safe and cosy. When it was crusted up, we'd break off pieces and dip them in olive oil and *za'atar*. It was soul food for Mum, who was so far away from her home and family.

I started making my own curtains and cushion covers with the sewing skills Reem and my mother had taught me. I couldn't wait until we had guests and I could say, 'Yes, I made those.' We'd set the wedding date for the end of the footy season in September 2000. Football was finishing early that year as the National Rugby League (NRL) shifted its season by a month so it didn't clash with the Olympics. But then in July I came home one day and Dad told me his old boss overseas had offered him work in Saudi Arabia for the next few months. After so much disappointment trying to find a regular, steady job it was an offer he couldn't refuse.

After telling me, Dad called Hazem and his family and asked them to join us one evening to discuss postponing the wedding for a few more months. None of us was happy about it as our home was ready and we'd already waited so long. But Dad was in a tough situation; he couldn't let that opportunity go as things were still grim on the job front in Sydney. Reem had become engaged to Akheel and they were planning their wedding for December. Dad assured us he would fly back for our weddings if we had them at the same time.

We all came to the agreement that it was just too long for Hazem and I to wait and so we decided to have the wedding before he left. That gave us less than a fortnight to put it all together. This was a big task, but the good thing was my dress and Hazem's suit were ready and to me that's all that we needed. My dress was made by the same friend who made my engagement dress. This time it was a classic ivory satin full gown with a pearl-encrusted boatneck. The pearls clustered at the neckline and scattered all the way down the bustline, with the three-quarter-length sleeves trimmed with more pearls. To me it was an Audrey Hepburn dress, classically elegant.

I had never been keen on big parties and weddings, enjoying more personal and intimate gatherings with close family and friends. That's how I wanted our wedding to be, so I wasn't unhappy that circumstances prescribed a small gathering. In such a short time there was no way Hazem and I could have organised a big wedding. Thankfully, Hazem shared my view. Both our parents received many enquiries from keen people who wanted to invite themselves just so they could say they were going to Hazem El Masri's wedding. The whole community was buzzing as they wanted to see the girl who'd won Hazem's heart. We decided to have the reception in our new home with close family and friends. Of course my dear friend Abeer was there.

There was a lot to do in a short time. Traditionally, at the reception the bride and groom are seated on a raised stage so all the guests can see the happy couple, but we had no way of organising one to fit in our formal lounge. But my mother, always the artistic innovator, said, 'We will build one!' She gathered all she needed and set about putting together a fancy platform in the centre of our new home. She sewed a matching backdrop which she pinned perfectly late one evening a few days before the ceremony. I love that about my mum, there is no obstacle she cannot overcome.

Of course Mum made my bridal bouquet. She chose mostly winter flowers, dusty pink and white tulips, white arum lilies and white tiger lilies, which she grew in our front yard. They grew alongside a jasmine bush that reminded her of her home in Syria. In full bloom in summer the jasmine perfume would fill the house and greet whoever was knocking at the door. When most other flowers have already bloomed, the lilies rise and grace winter in the most beautiful way. Flowers remind me so much of women, delicate and beautiful in all shapes, sizes and scents. Some are prickly and others fragile, but all are resilient and graceful, pushing through the earth to spring to life. You find them nearly everywhere on fruit trees and vegetables, on herb bushes and prickly pears – each flower a future fruit carrying the seeds of the next generation.

Sunday, 9 July 2000 was our wedding day. Hazem flew back to Sydney that morning after the Bulldogs had played the Melbourne Storm in Melbourne the day before. I woke up early and headed off with Mum to get my hair and makeup done. When I got home everyone was rushing around getting ready, Dad, my sisters and brothers and Hindiya. I went into my room to rest my eyes for a few minutes before Hazem arrived and we headed out to have photographs taken. Sitting on my bed, I looked around my room and suddenly realised that after tonight I was not going to be living with my parents or sleeping in my bed anymore, the bed I had slept in since a child. Everything was going to be different. My mother came into my room and sat down beside me. She opened her hand and said, 'I want you to have this.' She was holding the 21-carat gold bracelet that Hindiya had given her on her wedding.

I was surprised and said, 'Mum, this is yours!'

She replied, 'And now it's yours. Remember that you will always have a home here.' We hugged and I had to stop myself from crying too hard. We both knew that life was changing for both of us. Hindiya came in and Mum helped me into my dress and pinned my wedding veil and tiara while Hindiya watched. I was about to become a married woman.

That was it, there was no 'sex talk'. I was the first among my sisters to marry, but I don't think any of us had a conversation with our mother about what would happen on our wedding night. Mum is an educated and intelligent woman but she didn't feel comfortable talking to me about sex. I can understand her hesitation. I am sure I will feel the same when my daughters are older, but I will deal with any awkwardness it might bring. Islam teaches us that a mother and father have a duty to explain and guide their children in this aspect of life.

While writing this book I asked every older woman I knew well enough from many different religions and backgrounds how their own mother had addressed this issue when they were getting married. The answer was nearly always the same. Every woman had someone, if not her mother then a grandmother, an aunt, a sister, a cousin or trusted family friend, one of a network of women who talked to her if their mother had been too embarrassed to do it herself. This is not for unreasonable reasons but as an unspoken preservation of a vital mother–daughter relationship that is there for life. We see our mothers every day, they know so much about us and it may have been hard to overcome that awkwardness.

When I think back I realise that if my mother had had that conversation with me it would have changed our relationship. Though she had nurtured me, for Mum to address what I was about to experience could have had one of two outcomes – it could have brought us closer or pushed us apart. I think Mum chose not to take that chance and to preserve our relationship – she had always felt that slight distance between us. But I didn't go without such advice – my gorgeous grandmother Hindiya was there for me. She had the most careful conversation with me that day, making sure not to embarrass me. With her charming humour she put me at ease as I listened. By the end of that conversation I realised she knew a lot more than I thought she did.

I love my mother dearly and I am glad she gave that responsibility to Hindiya. Since I've married and had children my mother and I have become very close. I call her every day, sometimes twice a day, even about silly little things, just to hear her voice and see if she needs anything or to make sure she's okay. Mum spent most of her life away from her own mother, Hindiya, and I know how much she missed her presence. Today I try to make the most of the privilege of having my mother just a short drive away.

Hazem's and my wedding was the small, intimate ceremony we'd both wanted and it was shared with the most important people in our lives. As we had already performed the Islamic marriage ceremony this was now the party, with music and food. Ours was not the lavish event that I used to see unfold outside our apartment in Saudi Arabia, but the sense of celebration and generous serving of food was the same. Our guests ate an array of Lebanese dishes carefully selected by Amal – rice, lamb and tabouli with a range of sweets for all tastebuds alongside the wedding cake. There was so much food I'm sure no one went away hungry. When it was time to go our families and guests said goodbye as we headed out to the car for a drive to the city. When we returned some time later all the guests were gone and Hazem's family had packed all the mess away. Hazem and I were alone in our own home. I was now Arwa El Masri. Although it was something I didn't plan for, I have thought many times about changing back to my maiden name, keeping it as my mother had kept hers. Islam teaches that a woman is required to keep her maiden name in a marriage.

I needed to shower and undo my hair that was pinned up full of hairspray, but as I got into the shower and ran the hot water it was ice cold. I called out to Hazem and he went straight outside and found that the hot water system had broken down. I was waiting for him to come back and I could hear him buzzing in the kitchen. He grabbed every pot he could find, filled them up with water, heated them on the stove and brought them to me so I could at least have some warm water to rinse my long hair. Of course I will not discuss our first moments as husband and wife. They are sacred to me as they are to most of us. But what I will say is that Hazem is a gentleman in every respect.

The next day Hazem woke up at seven o'clock in the morning, got dressed, kissed me goodbye and went to training. None of his teammates knew he'd been married over the weekend; we kept it to ourselves because of the rush we were in to plan it before my father left. I also wasn't ready to be thrust into a football lifestyle and environment. It needed to be a transition and one that would come in due time. But no matter what I did to prepare myself nothing could have prepared me for what I was about to experience.

I decided to take some time off from my university studies and casual job at the home furnishings to settle into marriage with Hazem. He had a busy football and training schedule and I wanted to give my new life and role a chance to flourish and grow, without us both rushing around. I knew that our first year of marriage was going to be a big learning curve for both of us. Knowing someone and loving them can be very different to living with them and seeing them every day. We both wanted to have a solid foundation that would last for all the years to come. In my opinion the first year of marriage is a crucial time, it throws everything at you and, for a woman especially, it can shake your sense of self. If you persevere and treat each other with respect you set the tone of a marriage. That is something hard to do in busy lives, scrambling to snatch time together. With that in mind I made the decision to start my young married life as a homemaker. Hazem didn't object, he was happy if I was happy.

We were lucky we could afford to do this because we both were content with having enough. We didn't need a lot of money to be content. I wanted the privilege of waking up in the morning and not having to go to work or university; I had worked for a long time while I was studying and many times found the balance impossible to keep, with my family commitments and Dad's absences. One thing always suffered. I wanted to take care of my new home, I wanted to learn how to manage a household and I wanted to plant that vegetable patch I always dreamed of. To me it was still an education, an education about life not only for me but for the both of us. Hazem's job meant I could do all that if I wanted to, even though we were still paying off the house and were carefully managing our money.

I liked nothing more than cooking for Hazem and loved it when people came to visit so I could feed them too. I introduced *kabsa* to Hazem and his family; they loved it and had never tasted it before. I cooked traditional Middle Eastern foods that I learned from my mother but Amal taught me some too. She showed me the authentic way to make some Lebanese dishes Hazem loved: *Lahm bi Ajeen, fatoush* and tabouli salads and many more. I cooked modern Australian dishes and two of Hazem's favourites were creamy chicken and mushroom pasta and Aussie shepherd's pie.

I began to plan what I would plant in my vegetable patch. Eggplant is one of my most loved vegetables; it's so versatile and aromatic when roasted. I had started a recipe book while I was still at my parents' house. Reem had learned the art of binding books and as an engagement gift she gave me a blank book she had made. It was covered with the most beautiful fabric. I asked Mum and Hindiya for the recipes we all loved to eat so I could write them into this book. From traditional dishes to new and multicultural dishes I'd picked up along the way, I began an education in food. I read books and watched anything I could on cooking. I learned so much from local and international chefs who cherish the old and value the new way of cooking. I tested recipes in my kitchen and had many successes and also many failures. I mixed traditional with new until I found that perfect balance. I still have that book and I am still adding to it. I'm no expert but I did my best to introduce different foods to my children, educating their minds and palates as I go along. I can't wait until my children ask me how to make that special dish they love so much.

In that first year of marriage Hazem and I discovered many things about each other, but one thing I learned about him shocked me to the core: he hated eggplant! How could that be? I am a lover of anything with eggplants – fried, roasted, even pickled! I had already planned in my head how I was going to cook Hazem my favourite eggplant dish: oven-roasted or deep-fried baby eggplants filled with mince and pine nuts in a tomato base, in Arabic it's called *munazala*.

Before I knew about Hazem's aversion I had begun to sketch out that vegetable patch and I told Hazem one evening that I had it all sorted. I mentioned eggplants as one of the things I would plant and he said, 'I don't like eggplants, I don't eat them.'

'You mean roasted or fried?' I said, not understanding.

'I don't like them at all, I can't stand them in any way, their smell and flavour, I don't even like the way they look.' Something I loved was something he despised and he wasn't prepared to try it even once, not even for my sake. I folded. I made the first compromise in our marriage and didn't plant any eggplants in that vegetable patch. Middle Eastern food uses eggplants in many dishes, in my opinion it is a vegetable that cannot be replaced with another. Its flavour and texture is unique. Hazem still doesn't eat it and I didn't cook eggplants for the first few years of my marriage, not because he asked me not to but out of consideration to him. When I really missed eggplant I prepared it when he wasn't around, so the smell was gone by the time he came home – just as Amal had done when he was still at home. His comfort was important to me and mine to him. These days he is willing to put up with the smell of cooking eggplants for me.

Life is full of compromises and, in a marriage, to make things work they need to be made by both sides. If we try and see things through the eyes of the other person, even for a moment, that compromise becomes easier to make.

I planted our vegie patch with oregano and basil, tomatoes and Lebanese cucumbers, and I watched them grow every day, the miracle of life right before my eyes. That vegetable patch, especially the cucumber vine, would be a big part of my reason for deciding to wear my veil.

Hazem and I spent many nights in front of the fireplace talking and enjoying married life, warming up some Arab bread like my mother had in Grafton while the teapot boiled beside it. We would share that cosy experience with our families as we all got to know each other even better.

When Hazem and I were together we would talk and he'd make me laugh as he would share with me some of his schoolboy antics. Not many people know this about Hazem, but he is a true practical joker; I know this as I have been on the receiving end often, as have his football mates. We decided during one of these evenings that as soon as he was done with his football season, we'd head to Thredbo for a break. Straight after the last game of the year we packed our things and got in the car and drove for five and a half hours to get there.

We had both seen snow before. Lebanon is famous for its snow-topped mountains so Hazem had a strong memory, but neither of us had been to the snow as adults and I had never even touched it. We made no bookings, we just drove there and took things as they came. That's one of the beauties of being a newlywed – you can have a thought and just pack up and go! When we arrived we decided to stay in Jindabyne. It was evening when we arrived and I couldn't see any snow but it was very cold. The woman at the reception desk at the hotel told us she had only one room left so we were lucky. But then she told us it was near the end of the snow season for that year and that we shouldn't expect snowfall by tomorrow. I was disappointed and hoped that Allah would do something spectacular with his nature for us just this one time. We went to sleep hoping for a miracle.

As day broke I got out of bed, looked out the window and our car was covered with snow. The whole town was white. It was a breathtaking sight. I woke Hazem and we got dressed and walked outside. I knelt down and with my bare hands touched snow for the first time in my life. It felt so soft and strange. I rolled up a ball and called out to Hazem as I threw it at him. He had beat me to it and gathered up an even bigger snowball and got me with it first. We were like kids, laughing and having a good time. The woman from the hotel came out to us and said, 'You know you're lucky! It hasn't snowed in Jindabyne for a while.' It was a miracle and a blessing that I will never forget.

We went up to the mountain that day and tried many things but our favourite was the toboggan. We laughed so hard as we both went flying off the end of it into the soft carpet of fresh snow. Winter is so beautiful, everything is hidden under the fallen snow and it is all serene. What some call the season of death is remarkably peaceful and graceful. Hazem and I sat together looking out at a blanket of white as we sipped on hot chocolates. Australia really is a remarkable continent; with all its different environments it is unique. From snowy mountains to a red desert, lush green rainforests and beaches, to arid sandy dunes for miles, the reefs and bush, the more I see of it, the more I want to see. When we returned home from that trip we promised ourselves to go back again, but the busyness of life has kept us from doing that so far.

In the first few months of our marriage we would have a lot of visitors coming to congratulate us on our union. Most of them were Hazem's friends; they would visit with their wives hoping the two wives would hit it off and become good friends like the husbands. I would have been happy to make new friendships but it didn't happen often. I don't think I am demanding, all I look for in a friend is a good heart and a willingness to exchange ideas and thoughts about life. Sadly, many of the women seemed more interested in Hazem than in me . . . except for two. Mona and Fida and I hit it off right away and we became friends. They were special: they didn't want to know me just for Hazem's sake or to be able to say that they socialise with us.

I have always been very selective with my friendships, and consider myself a good judge of character when it comes to people's sincerity. That came in very handy once I married Hazem, but it also took a toll. As Hazem became more and more successful on the football field he became like a trophy to collect. It amazed me how pushy some people could be trying to get near him. For a while I was affected quite strongly by people's intrusive natures. It seemed there were some who wanted to know everything about our lives and they delighted in gossiping about me and Hazem even though they knew nothing about us. That pushed me into a deep depression and I became quite isolated. Hazem was the first Muslim sporting star in Australia and so there was no one I could talk to in our community for advice. We were the first and had to figure things out on our own. We both worked it out together and came to terms with it. We met many lovely people because of football. Passers-by and well-wishers have stopped us many times in the streets to tell us how much they like and respect Hazem and they will never be forgotten. The hundreds of pieces of fan mail he received will be there for his children to read one day.

I had to deal with the fact I was now married to a sportsman who, no matter how decent he was, had a label attached to him. As a footballer it was assumed he was only interested in a woman who was sexy and beautiful to look at regardless of her brain – in other words, a trophy wife. Even I had made the same sort of stereotypical judgment when my girlfriend asked me to help her interview Hazem years before; I had quickly realised how wrong I was but it didn't make it any easier for me now. Our connection was based on respect and deep love for one another, but I knew others questioned it and it bothered me a great deal. I hate any sort of prejudice and I think it is demeaning to label women who are in relationships with sportsmen as 'WAGS' (Wives and Girlfriends). I had never heard that term until one of my fellow 'wagettes' told me years later. The media lump all these women into a group that is assumed to be full of designer-label-wearing bimbos and gold-diggers only concerned with trivial matters such as their appearance. Such labels and preconceptions are insulting to any wife or girlfriend.

Most of the women I have met who are married to or going out with footballers are a long way from this description. Sure, many like to look good (who doesn't?), but once I made the leap to get to know them I discovered a fabulous, diverse and multi-talented group of women. Women who are in this position have their relationships dissected in the public arena and have their love for their men questioned, with all eyes looking at them all the time. I don't deny that there are those around the periphery of any sport who want a trophy man, but from my experience these women don't tend to have long-term relationships. It seems as if many wonder, *Why is he with her and not me? I wonder what he sees in her?* How terrifying to have to prove your love or intentions to others about something so personal. I wasn't ever prepared to do that and was glad to keep my engagement to Hazem a secret from most until we were married. It saved me from a lot of scurrilous gossip.

It takes a strong and brave woman to be with someone who is famous because it is a constantly intrusive and testing life. People think they know you, and everything about you is thought to be in the public interest. You will be to some extent defined by your husband's or boyfriend's achievements and success and that was something I wasn't at all prepared for. I am always proud of Hazem's achievements. I have been a part of how hard he worked to get to where he is. I watched him pack his bags to go to a game over three hundred times, I watched him take the field over three hundred times and I nursed his wounds over three hundred times. Every tackle, every kick I shared with him aged me as the number of grey hairs on my head grew. But I wasn't alone. Hazem's network of women who supported him throughout his career were right there with me, from his mother to his three sisters and now his daughters, sharing that sideline stress.

As proud as I am of my husband, I'm also a proud woman who refuses to walk in the shadow of a successful man. Neither of us stand alone – we are one. But everything my parents strived to empower me with, to have the ability to stand on my own two feet and not have my existence as a female be defined by the man in my life, was tested because of the public perceptions of a woman married to a sportsman. It took some time for me to come to terms with it all and to realise, ultimately, it didn't matter what others thought of me. I knew that Hazem and I were equals in our relationship and that the way we chose to live was no one's business but ours. But in the early days I felt different. I thought I was the only one who felt this way and didn't socialise with the football wives right away. I would sit in the general crowd with Hazem's brothers and sisters. Even when we were married, no one on his team knew we were there until the season began the following year. That gave us the space to find our own way, out of the limelight.

The first time I went as Hazem's wife to watch him play I met a few of his teammates and something happened I will never forget. Darren Smith is one of rugby league's gentlemen and I had always admired the way he played alongside Hazem. There was almost an unspoken communication between the two both on and off the field. His reputation for being an all-round respectable, nice guy preceded him and I was looking forward to getting to know him. Hazem introduced him to me and, being a gentleman, he put his hand out to shake my hand but I couldn't oblige. I raised my hand to my chest and said, 'I'm sorry, I can't shake your hand, Darren.' I could see his surprise as he pulled his hand back and apologised as though he had offended me. He hadn't. I was the one who was embarrassed to make him feel that way.

I was upset by the whole experience, especially because it happened in front of a group of people and I wished I had explained better that Islam prohibits physical contact between men and women who are not married. That means anything from a handshake to a kiss hello is not permitted, but it is okay to shake hands with other women. The rules in this matter are the same for both men and women. This rule is regardless of race or religion, even Hazem's brothers don't shake my hand.

And that's how I explain it to anyone who offers their hand in kindness, so they don't think it's something personal or a rejection to their welcome.

I have had that situation happen many times throughout my life, and especially since being married to Hazem. I have had to decline shaking hands with lovely people in the local park, government ministers and big company CEOs, reporters and photographers, stars and legends from all walks of life. Since that moment with Darren I have learned to explain and to put people at ease about it. Any awkwardness disappears when I smile and continue to talk with them. Many people are unaware of this aspect of a woman's life in Islam and they are intrigued and walk away happier that they now know something new about Islam.

Munazala (mince-stuffed baby eggplants in tomato base)

Ingredients

2 kg long baby eggplants
1 tbs butter
1 brown onion, chopped
250g lean lamb mince
1 tsp salt
½ tsp ground cinnamon
¼ tsp ground black pepper
½ tsp ground pimento
1 × 400g can tomato puree
½ cup water
500ml sunflower oil for frying eggplants
½ tsp salt and ½ tsp pepper for the puree

Method

Wash and peel the baby eggplants removing one section of the black skin then leaving the next, creating a zebra stripe pattern. With a knife make a cut in the centre of the eggplant (the rounder section) creating a small pocket or pouch to fill in with the mince. Heat up the oil and deep fry them until slightly golden in colour. Drain on paper towel.

In a separate frypan melt the butter, add the chopped onion and sauté until translucent. Then add the mince and allow to cook through. Add all the spices and mix well.

After allowing the eggplants to drain carefully open the pouch and fill with the cooked mince (approximately one tablespoon). Place the stuffed eggplants in a deep oven dish and arrange them with the meat pocket facing up.

Mix the tomato puree and water with the salt and pepper and pour around and over the eggplants. Place in a hot oven (200°C) and bake for 30 to 40 minutes. Sprinkle with toasted pine nuts and enjoy with Arab bread.

Serves 6 to 8 people.

Tabouli salad

Ingredients

　　3 small bunches flat-leaf parsley
　　¼ cup burghul, washed and drained
　　3 firm tomatoes
　　6 spring onions
　　1 bunch fresh mint
　　3 leaves of cos lettuce, chopped very finely
　　2 tsp salt (or to taste)
　　1 tsp dried mint leaves
　　½ tsp sumac
　　¼ cup lemon juice
　　Zest of 1 lemon
　　¼ cup extra virgin olive oil
　　A few leaves of baby cos lettuce for serving

Method

Chop the parsley finely and wash and drain well. Place in the fridge, covered, for an hour to help dry out the remaining moisture. Wash and clean the burghul well and allow it to dry slightly.

Chop the tomatoes finely along with the spring onions and washed mint leaves and add the finely chopped cos lettuce leaves (this helps lighten the salad). Add the chopped parsley and mix well. Add the rest of the ingredients and mix.

Fill each lettuce leaf with a scoop of tabouli and place the parcels on a serving tray. This salad is best enjoyed with barbecued kebabs.

Serves 4 to 6 people.

Chapter Eleven
The World Keeps Turning

I loved my married life and focused my energy on my home, on cooking, and tending my vegie patch. As spring came around the plants burst with life, the herbs thrived and the tomatoes were red and juicy, but it was the cucumber vine that would impress me the most. I watched the flowers lock and turn into small wombs, then within a few days miraculously transform into the smallest baby cucumbers. I was so thrilled to watch them grow a little more day by day. One Friday morning I called my mother for our early morning chat. I had got into the habit of calling her around the same time every day. We'd talk as we both sipped coffees. Mum and I are early birds, when I still lived at home I would come down the stairs and find her waiting for me at the kitchen table with a cup of fresh coffee. We would chat and catch up on things that were happening in our week. I made an effort to continue our morning chats over the phone.

On this day I told her how my cucumbers were coming along nicely. Mum told me to get a ruler and measure one of them. I asked her why and she said to measure one early in the morning and then just before sunset to see how much it had grown in a day. I was sceptical, surely it couldn't grow with any noticeable length in a few hours. I hung up the phone and went straight out to the garden and measured the cucumber at 6.5 centimetres. I marked it with a ribbon and went inside. As I was making lunch I turned on the radio and listened to the Friday sermon being delivered by the imam. It was about being a true Muslim who practises Islam correctly, one who is strong at heart and not afraid of being committed to Allah. Something in me stirred. I knew my heart was always ready to take my faith to the next level, but I didn't think I was strong enough to face a society that might not accept me because I wore a veil. It was something that was always on my mind; no matter how much I ignored it, it always found a way back in. That day Allah was calling me.

I finished listening to the sermon and then went on with my day, doing a bit of housework and then baking Dad's favourite orange cake to share with Hazem. I almost forgot to go back out to the garden. The sun was beginning to set and just before the light disappeared completely I went back out to measure the cucumber. I took that same ruler and measured it: this time the cucumber was seven centimetres long. It had grown half a centimetre in half a day! I measured twice to be sure. I was in awe, I couldn't believe it was possible and when I stood up something in me had changed. I felt an inner strength I had never felt before. It might sound odd but the only way I can explain it is I now felt a connection to the earth I was standing on, I almost felt it moving under my feet. I realised something I already knew, that there are miracles happening around us every day, we are just oblivious to them most of the time. Whether we notice them or not, they are happening many times without human intervention. Like clockwork, the world keeps turning, generations come and go and no one knows when and where they will die. Was I going to live my life being afraid of what people thought about me or worry how people would treat me if I was visibly Muslim?

At that moment I was free of any anxiety about other people's expectations. My only concern should be my family and my commitment to Allah. Wearing the hijab, my veil, was a way of honouring that commitment and showing my respect for Islam. I walked into the house and went to get ready to go out with Hazem, as we were visiting friends that evening. I was in my bedroom and I pulled out a veil Reem and I had made together when she was teaching me to sew. I folded it and a rush of memory hit me. I closed my eyes and could see myself as a young girl in Saudi Arabia pinning my veil on my head before I went to school. As I threw the fabric over my hair, it was like it was yesterday. I felt completely at peace and pinned it right in my first attempt. It was like riding a bike, you never forget how it's done. I walked out and Hazem had just got home. He looked at me, smiled and said, 'Looks nice, are you ready to go?'

I said yes and he asked me if I was going like that. I said, 'It's staying.' He gave me the biggest smile. I saw in his eyes that he was proud of me, he hugged me and a tear rolled down my cheek. Hazem knew I was ready, he could see it in my eyes.

Since that day I have never looked back. I am as confident about my decision to wear the hijab today as ever. It was my choice and my connection to Allah that gave me the courage to wear it. I just wish I had done it sooner. At that moment I wished my parents hadn't made that difficult decision to bring us to Australia without it.

The veil is a life commitment that a Muslim woman chooses. It is not only a cover for your hair; it means much more than that. The veil also protects the modesty of a woman's dress. A woman's clothing should cover her body and not be see-through or tight fitting; any of these things negate the intention implicit in wearing a veil. But a woman does not wear the veil in her own home unless there are male visitors to the house. If I am with women I do not wear it. When I train at my local gym, which is for women only, I wear gym gear like everyone else. On a hot day, cooking in my kitchen I would not wear the veil, I wear a singlet or t-shirt like everyone else. The easiest way to explain when a woman is required to wear the veil is if she will be in the presence of a man who is not a blood relative, a man who at one time could be a potential suitor. I do not have to wear the veil in front of Hazem or his father but I do wear it around his brothers.

In my opinion there is a great deal of misinformation about the veil and both Muslims and non-Muslims are often confused about what it means. It is not merely a piece of fabric that covers a woman's hair, it represents a woman's right to be seen as more than just a sexual being; it shows that she refuses to be judged on physical attributes alone. Judaism, Christianity and Islam have all referenced the veil for women in their holy texts. They all explain that the purpose of these veils was not so much to obscure as it is to shield. In Christianity the Virgin Mary is always portrayed as a veiled woman. Throughout history, regardless of religion or nationality, committed devout women are represented in various images of being veiled. What many people regard as primitive or outdated is to my mind a simple way for a woman to protect herself against unwanted objectionable sexual attention in a world that sexualises women.

Choosing to wear the veil for me is a feminist decision. I didn't choose it only because I was required as a woman in Islam, I did it because I believe in it. After careful thought and a constant questioning about my place in the world and a questioning of the position of *all* women in society I chose it for what it stands for. I didn't look for my rights as a woman in the feminist movement; I looked for them within Islam and what I found is that feminism exists in Islam. I have seen and felt the difference of being a woman with and without a veil.

I have always dressed conservatively so not much about my dress sense had changed, I just added the right colour hijab to match my outfit. I continued to shop where everyone else did. There are many shops who design clothing only for veiled women, which can be quite traditional, but in recent years there has been an increase in Muslim women designers in Australia who have managed to blend the two: a contemporary modesty in outfits that are beautiful and stylish. But there were some things that did change. I now had to find a hairdresser who catered for Muslim women; that meant having a private room away from the shopfront window. Many people have asked me if having a hijab means I don't colour or cut my hair, or having my legs covered means that I don't wax. Islam encourages a woman to take care of herself in these matters. Just because everyone can't see my body doesn't mean it's neglected or unmaintained.

I will teach my daughters all I know about the hijab and educate them about what it means and what kind of commitment it takes to wear it; but it will be their choice to wear it and no one else's. I often find my daughter Lamya looking in my things and pinning one of my veils on her head pretending to be me, and when she says to me, 'Mum, can I wear it too?' my answer to her is: 'When you're old enough and ready for it I will buy you your own.'

My two older sisters and many of my close Muslim friends have chosen not to wear the hijab and that to me is their choice, as it was for me. I don't believe that because a woman chooses not to wear the hijab that she is in any way less committed to Allah.

I was so completely comfortable with my decision to assume the veil that the first time I walked out in public wearing my veil was a complete shock to me. Straightaway I could see people looking at me differently, as though I didn't belong here, as if I were a stranger and had just arrived from another country. There were whispers and lingering stares that I knew were because of my hijab as I had never noticed them before. I remembered the many times out with Abeer and how she was looked at when we were together. One of the reasons I had hesitated in wearing the veil was the way people would react, so on one level I had expected this, but on another it saddened me because these reactions were based on prejudice not on the person I was. I was still the same person and the manner with which I dealt with others was the same as it had always been.

The first time I went to one of Hazem's football matches with his brothers and sisters as a veiled woman we watched the game and waited for the crowd to leave before heading to the tunnel to make our way to the car in the VIP parking. Hazem had given me all the necessary passes to get through to the authorised areas. As I made my way to the gate a female guard was staffing the entrance to the tunnel. As soon as I got close she started to shout at me and waved her hands gesturing no before speaking in slow, drawn-out English, 'You . . . can't . . . come . . . this . . . way! You . . . have . . . to . . . go . . . the . . . other . . . way! You . . . need . . . to . . . have . . . a special . . . pass . . . do you . . . UNDERSTAND?'

I just looked at her in amazement, opened my wallet and handed over the passes. 'Which do you want?' I asked. 'This one? This one? Or these?'

The World Keeps Turning

The woman was red-faced and moved back quickly as she realised she had been rude. I said nothing more and passed straight through.

Once I started wearing the hijab this type of situation happened a lot; people assumed that I didn't speak English. I found out that this is very common if someone looks ethnically different. My mother had struggled with a different aspect of this because she did have limited English, but because of that she was sometimes treated as if she also had limited intelligence. She may have battled with English but the nuances of a person's behaviour when dealing with her told my mother plenty.

Being married to Hazem meant that I was going to attract attention anyway, but as soon as I chose to wear my veil I became a public ambassador for my religion without ever putting my hand up for the job. Because of my nature I am happy to discuss my religion, as most Muslims are, but there was now an added pressure. I wanted to make sure I was informed enough so when people were curious about the veil and about Islam I could answer confidently and in a way that was easy to understand. There was always a curiosity about my veil, but the events of September 11 rocked us all and people's views of Arabs and, in particular, Muslim Arabs were heightened and changed. The events of that day shocked and horrified everyone. I was in shock watching those towers fall, knowing mothers, fathers, sons and daughters were dying before our eyes. Islam prohibits the harm of innocent people and the actions of a few have marred every Muslim in the world. I think all religions have been dealt a terrible blow with all that is happening around us; people now associate being religious with being extreme or violent or hating others.

All religions from the beginning of time have at some stage been used as a front for people's own agendas and as an excuse for behaviour that is selfish. This was not the intention of the prophets, but the actions of some who have distorted their message after their passing. When holy texts are manipulated and misinterpreted by people to further their own needs this has a devastating ripple effect for centuries to come. How is it that a person's right to practise any faith they believe in has become offensive to others? It seems to have become 'taboo' to announce that you are religious these days; people's faith in God is something that others are offended at and don't want to hear about. This is a result of religion being used as a front for some political gains. Religion can become a shield and an excuse for people's actions no matter how wrong their motives are, so it is no wonder there is confusion and distrust of all faiths.

The concentration of the media on the actions of a few puts everyone of that faith, race or nationality in jeopardy. The misinformed then begin to draw opinions about millions of people because of the actions of a few hundred. The power of the press shapes public opinion and the minds of generations to come. Language is very powerful. For example, if you tell your child they are a liar repeatedly they will assume this habit in everything they do, just as they would if you had praised a positive behaviour. That is why I believe that there is no greater privilege than to be a mother, we are the first educators to our children who are the next generation. But the privilege to teach is not one that everyone is able to do successfully. It is a job more difficult to perform than any building project or space expedition; you are responsible for a living breathing human being.

Hazem was under great pressure as a Muslim in the public arena as many reacted to the horror of September 11 with anger and hate towards *every* Muslim person. He had many instances where people approached him to vent their frustration or fury at him. His football club, the Canterbury-Bankstown Bulldogs received death threats and were asked why they had a terrorist playing on their side. Even some of his teammates made it known they were finding it hard to understand why Hazem's religion encouraged these horrific acts. Hazem handled the pressure well and stayed true to himself. He knew that all he could do was to go on doing what he did best, lead by example and show he was a Muslim Australian who was proud of his country and his religion, and that hate was never a part of that equation.

I found myself in a strange new world and I did what I'd always done, I began to search for answers and I educated myself about my religion even more. I wanted to find the truth. I looked for old books that have been around for centuries, I read the Quran and books of the prophets – the *Hadith* and *Sunna*, that outline the Prophet Mohammed's practice and teachings. They gave me a sense of what Islam is truly all about. I also read books by scholars that are well known in both the Middle East and in the West: Ibn Sinna (Avicenna), Al-Tabari and the great traveller Ibn Battuta, to name a few. These Muslim teachers were spiritual philosophers and scientists, musicians and poets who linked the holy words of the Quran to the sciences of the world and everyday life. What I found was something I had known all along: that Islam teaches many things, but the most powerful lesson is that of peace and harmony.

The first words you say before reciting any passage of the Quran are 'In the name of Allah the most merciful the most compassionate' and to greet another person you say 'Peace be upon you'. How then can a religion that preaches such peace become the face of evil? It is not Islam that created such horror, it was a distortion. But in its coverage the media didn't care about portraying the majority of Muslims who live as Allah intended, and how the prophets taught, in peace and harmony. Most Muslims live their lives in the peaceful way that most of us do, caring for our families, our friends and our communities. The media focused on the tiny minority portrayed as angry bearded men and subservient veiled women who hated anything to do with Western society. As a veiled Muslim woman at this time, it was impossible not to feel isolated and inferior. But I did my best and kept on smiling, although it was very hard at times. I knew that for me patience was the only way. When people said to Hazem and me, 'Oh, you're not like them, you guys are different' I was pleased that I had helped open someone's eyes to the fact that Muslims are people like Hazem and me and that we are the norm not the exception.

After our first year of marriage I didn't go to the footy as often as I was getting ready to continue my studies. I had stayed at home for just over a year, and then, with Hazem's encouragement, I went back to university to complete my degree. Most of the students I had studied with had graduated, but I wondered if my teachers would remember me. When they last saw me I was a single woman, now I was a veiled married woman and I wasn't sure how they would react. One of the first classes I had when I went back was with Peter Skrzynecki and as soon as I entered his lecture room he smiled and said, 'Well, well, if it isn't quenched thirst.' He took one look at my veil and said, 'You look lovely.' He put me at ease right away and never mentioned it again.

The university was bustling with new students, and a lot had changed in a fairly short time. There were many veiled women at the campus, enrolled in a wide range of degrees, so I was no longer anxious about being one of a few, like Abeer was when we had first enrolled in 1996. There was now a Muslim students' group and a prayer room lined with carpet for students to pray, with a washroom right beside the entrance. I was delighted when I prayed there the first time in 2002. I remember Abeer and I walking all around the campus in our first year, looking for an empty clean room to pray in. When we found a room, one of us would stand at the door so no one walked in and interrupted our prayer. Then we'd swap. Noticing all these changes made me feel happy – it was a sign that there was a greater acceptance of difference and it further cemented the sense of belonging that had taken so long for me to find.

I enjoyed returning to university and my studies. It was even better the second time around because I felt I was able to understand things with more maturity. I had a more well-rounded view of issues that I was certain were so wrong before. I realised it wasn't only the university that was different, I was too. And I was about to change again . . . in the most wonderful way!

I was so busy juggling university and home life and supporting Hazem's football career that I didn't realise I had missed one of my periods. When I did I was anxious and told my mother. She knew I had been busy and that stress, good or bad, could affect a woman's cycle, so she suggested I wait for the next one and if it still hadn't arrived then I should visit the doctor for a blood test. I couldn't wait! I went out and bought a home pregnancy test and that evening I found out I was pregnant. I told Hazem the news and we were both excited and happy.

A few months earlier, when we had made the decision to start a family, I had fallen pregnant almost instantly, but I went through what most women describe as the most devastating experience any pregnant woman can have, no matter how far she is into her pregnancy. I had a miscarriage. I was devastated and the speed with which I went from hopeful, happy expectant mother to crying and shattered woman was disturbing. It was the single most horrible private experience of my female existence, to lose something that is living inside of you down a toilet was, in my mind, devastating. I began to doubt I would ever be able to carry a child. My doctor told me I wasn't alone, and the first pregnancy was the most common to lose.

His words didn't make things better, from that moment I was determined to fall pregnant again and the more we failed the sadder I became. I turned to Allah and asked him for peace as I knew he would guide me. I have never turned to Allah in prayer and walked away unfulfilled; my connection with Allah is strong and in my toughest times and darkest hour I felt his peace upon me and guidance to do what's right. I tried to look to the future and realised if that child was meant to survive it would still be here. There was a reason for everything. The minute we stopped concentrating on trying, I fell pregnant with our beautiful daughter Lamya. Hazem was on a trip away with the footy club when I found out and it was one of the happiest moments in my life when I called him with the good news.

That year of study would pass quickly; I sat for my final English exam when I was seven and a half months pregnant. Hazem was at the forefront of a new venture too. He was asked to play on the Australian–Lebanese team for the second time. The first time was a World Cup qualifier that took him to the USA and France during our engagement, but this time he was more determined to be involved because the team was going to Lebanon. Due to my pregnancy, I wasn't able to go too, but Hazem travelled to Lebanon for the first time in nearly fifteen years and his mother, Amal, and sister and brother went along too. They all had a great time seeing family they had missed dearly over the years. Hazem was back well before our first child was born.

On 13 January 2003 our daughter was born. Lamya was a beautiful baby and, if I close my eyes, I can still hear her first cry ringing in my ears. I never considered myself a maternal kind of woman, motherhood was something I had to prepare myself for. I read all the books I could get my hands on, I asked Mum all the questions I could think of, but when the doctor handed me my first child a fierce maternal instinct was born too. I felt almost like a dagger went straight through my heart that cut both ways and I was linked to her for life. If Lamya were happy or sad I was going to feel it. I turned to my mother instantly and asked her to forgive me if I had ever done anything that upset her at any time, as I now understood her love for us. No matter how over-protective it seemed to me at the time I suddenly knew where her fear and need to protect us came from.

Hazem's eyes welled up witnessing the birth of his first child and I could see that he, like me, had been struck by that unconditional love. Children are a gift and we are entrusted to look after them, Hazem and I take that responsibility very seriously. It is a child's basic human right to be healthy and safe and loved by a parent who provides that. The word mother is an important one. Some think all it means is to be able to bear children, I think not; many women can have children but sadly not every woman cares for that child well.

I felt comfortable in the responsibility of nurturing our child and welcomed the new role parenthood brought to our lives. I loved nothing more than looking after her and I cocooned us both at home for the first few weeks. The fact that my graduation ceremony was held soon after Lamya's birth was another sign that my world was changing.

I was sad that Hazem couldn't be there to see me in my gown receiving my degree but he had to be in New Zealand with the Bulldogs. That is the reality when you are married to an elite athlete, no matter how much he wants to be with his family at key moments the commitment to the sport and the team had to come first – to a degree. Peter Skrzynecki would join the ceremony along with my mother and sister Maha who looked after Lamya. Dad was overseas and couldn't get back but he called to congratulate me and I heard a great happiness in his voice. I was so proud to have finally completed my degree and so happy that people I cared about were there to see that achievement. But as I looked out at the audience I was distracted by what I considered an even greater achievement: I was a mother and I couldn't stop smiling at Lamya, who was far too young to realise what a big moment this was for her mum.

After graduation we went back to Mum's place and, as usual, she had cooked up a storm. She made all my favourite eggplant dishes: babaganoush and *munazala* to celebrate, which was the only good thing about Hazem not being there. I was a content and very happy mum who had just fulfilled my parents' and my own dream – I had my university degree.

Dad's favourite orange cake

Ingredients

- 125g unsalted butter, chopped
- 2 tbs grated orange rind
- 1 tbs lemon zest
- 1 tsp vanilla bean paste
- ¾ cup sugar
- 2 eggs
- 1½ cups self-raising flour
- ⅓ cup fresh orange juice
- ½ cup milk

Method

Grease a Baba cake pan and dust with flour. Heat the oven to a moderate temperature (180°C). Combine all the ingredients in a bowl and mix with an electric beater on slow. After a few minutes mix on high until the mixture changes in colour (it may appear curdled at this stage but it will reconstitute).

Pour in cake pan and bake for 40 minutes. Allow the cake to cool for 5 minutes then turn onto a wire rack.

Before cake is completely cool place on a serving plate or in a storage container and cover to allow it to stay moist. Spread with orange marmalade and enjoy with a cup of tea.

Serves 6 to 8 people.

Babaganoush

Ingredients

- 2 large eggplants
- 1 tsp salt (or to taste)
- ⅓ cup lemon juice
- 2 garlic cloves, crushed
- Zest of 1 lemon
- ¼ cup of Tahina
- Drizzle of extra virgin olive oil and chopped parsley for presentation

Method

Wash and clean eggplants well. Using a knife pierce a straight line down the centre of the eggplant, not separating the pieces, then again on the opposite side creating four attached quarters (the eggplant should still look whole). Place on a tray and brown under griller turning it as each side cooks, this should take about 40 minutes.

Alternatively bake on an open gas flame barbecue or charcoal barbecue for best chargrilled flavour (cooking time may vary using these methods). When eggplants are cooked allow them to cool slightly then remove the flesh using your hands and discarding the skin.

Place into a bowl and add the salt, lemon juice, garlic, lemon zest and mix well, mashing the flesh well. Then add tahina and mix.

Place in a serving dish and drizzle with olive oil and top with chopped parsley.

For another way to serve, add the same ingredients except the tahina, place the eggplant mix on a serving dish, top with chopped walnuts and parsley, and drizzle with a little pomegranate molasses and olive oil.

Enjoy with Arab bread or chopped fresh vegetables or barbecued meats.

Serves 4 to 6 people.

Chapter Twelve
From Cedars to Gum Trees

Our sense of belonging is something no one can dictate to us, it is a matter of the heart. The old saying 'home is where the heart is' is a deeply profound statement that gets downgraded as cliché, but it's the simple truths that speak volumes.

I discovered this overwhelming sense of belonging when I travelled out of Australia for the first time since I arrived with my parents back in 1989. In the spring of 2003 Hazem was again chosen to travel to Lebanon to play football in the Mediterranean Cup and Lamya and I were going with him. This game was special as Hazem's brother Wissam would be playing beside his big brother in Lebanon while Amal and I watched in the crowd. It was a wonderful experience to travel with him to see all the places he remembered as a child and to meet his extended family. We visited places in Lebanon that seemed so familiar and close to my heart although I had never been there before. Surprisingly, there were familiar sounds and smells that evoked a memory that I didn't realise was so strong.

Lebanon is a popular tourist destination for travellers from the Middle East and from around the world. Its majestic land and its extremes are breathtaking. It is famous for its cedar forests and mountainous terrain. You can visit a cave at the top of the mountains with icicles hanging from the ceiling, then drive down the valley to the hottest seashore spotted with sunbaking bodies.

We arrived in Beirut in an early evening in October 2003. Lamya was only nine months old but she proved to be a good traveller. There was another traveller as well, but we didn't know it yet. I was carrying our second child, Zayd. As we were greeted at the airport by Hazem's uncle the unmistakable blood link was in his eyes. Nothing about his features resembled Hazem, but the way he blinked and turned his head in shyness was just like Haz.

As dusk fell over the city we drove out of Beirut to Hazem's home city of Tripoli, which was an hour or so away. I pinned my forehead to the window trying to see as much as I could before the light disappeared. The geography of Lebanon is remarkable, mountains with snow tops and hills of green and cedar trees as far as the eye can see. Then suddenly there is a deep valley where the mountain meets the sea. The Mediterranean sea cradles so many countries that are so different yet similar. I began to wonder if the waves that were hitting the coastline in Lebanon right before my eyes would, in a few hours, travel down and hit the shores of Palestine. How I wished I was a wave in that sea, to see the holy land even for a moment.

We arrived at the apartment we were staying in, which was on the tenth floor, and I opened a window to see the city glistening with lights. I could look down and see people talking on the street and I breathed in the air, wanting all my senses to absorb the city Hazem was born in. He stood beside me looking out on the city of his childhood memories – memories of happiness and pain. Hazem had witnessed his beloved country become devastated by a war that lasted decades. His experiences as a child were very different from mine, he had to duck under bombs and hide in bunkers from the air assaults that were devastating his homeland. I could only imagine the horror of that for him and how desperate his parents must have been to get their children to safety. They arrived in Australia as war refugees and left behind everything to raise their family away from war. I would have done the same – I would risk everything to protect my children if I had to.

I found it hard to sleep that night because I was too excited. I couldn't wait to meet Hazem's family, see his old home where he grew up, visit his old school and the mosque he used to visit with his father and uncles as a young boy. Finally my eyes shut for a few hours and to my delight I was woken by a sound echoing through the city – it was the call to prayer from the local mosque. It is the most beautiful sound and, until I heard it, I didn't realise how much I'd missed it. In a few moments the city woke with men and women on their way to prayer and work. In all my excitement I popped my head out the window and forgot my veil. I could see the fruit and vegetable trolleys filling the main street and heard another familiar sound, a man's voice calling out, 'Cucumbers . . . cucumbers . . . sweet fresh cucumbers.' I felt a tear roll down my cheek and a hand on my back, it was Hazem watching me; the vendor's voice had stirred memories for us both.

As I walked down the street with Hazem later that morning I studied every small detail I saw – faces and people, old streets and the buildings that had withstood the war. We walked past shops and stalls and I could smell the produce from metres away. There were tomatoes that tasted like tomatoes and the addictive smell of freshly baked Arab bread. The mouth-watering smell got to us and we stopped at a bakery, ordered some bread then tore pieces off it and ate it in the middle of the street. It was hot and delicious. We couldn't do things like that in Sydney because someone would always recognise Hazem and come up for a chat, or stand and watch him from a distance. We didn't mind people's attention generally, it was a nice thing most of the time and came with being a well-known footy player, but there were moments, like eating on the street, when you didn't want to be watched.

Being in Lebanon meant Hazem could walk through the streets anonymously like a normal person. It was refreshing . . . but it didn't last. We were walking through the shopping strip in Tripoli, Hazem was holding Lamya in his arms as we tried to cross a busy intersection when suddenly an Aussie-accented voice shouted out above all the street's noise. We both looked around but couldn't see who it was. All we could hear was 'El Masri!' getting louder as it got closer. Then an Aussie visiting Lebanon, who looked just like every other Lebanese man there, stepped up and said, 'Hey mate, what are you doing around here?' He chatted with Hazem at the side of the road, telling him he was on a working holiday visiting some family in Tripoli. When he left I asked Hazem how he knew the man, and he didn't. He was a league fan who had recognised Hazem amongst the crowd. Two Aussies on the streets of Tripoli having a conversation about rugby league, with the rest of the city going about its day. They looked so at home yet so out of place; everything about that moment was strangely beautiful.

We continued on our way and Hazem took me to his former home in the centre of Tripoli and we walked by the old barber shop where he used to get his hair cut. As we passed it Hazem saw that the man he knew was still working there. We walked in and Hazem said, '*Assalamu alaikum*' and gave the man a hug. He was puzzled but when Hazem explained who he was the barber broke out in the biggest smile and said, 'Your grandfather and uncles still come here and you look just like them, my son. Sit down and I'll give you a haircut for old time's sake.' So Hazem sat down in the same seat he had sat in as a child attended by the same barber – but in another lifetime. I could see in Hazem's eyes at that moment he was a young boy again.

After days filled with visiting family, eating delicious Lebanese food and mouth-watering seafood at night and sightseeing during the day, it was time for Hazem to get back to work. He was sharing some of Australia with the people of Lebanon. We watched Hazem's Mediterranean Cup games and the time flew by. Before I knew it he was playing in the finals against France.

I watched Hazem play the game he loved and was so proud of his talent. He was playing in front of a crowd of spectators who didn't know the rules of the game but who were cheering anyway for the Australian–Lebanese team. The stadium was a new and beautiful building, built in a city where poverty was still rife and so it was a stark contrast to many of the neglected neighbourhoods nearby. But that night it didn't matter, everyone was happy to be there. The grandstand was packed and they all cheered as Hazem ran out as captain of the Australian–Lebanese side with both Muslim and Christian players together as one. Team unity is the way that sport works; something sport in general is known for.

Sport had achieved what politics could not – or were they one and the same? In my opinion sport is a highly political arena, but one in which you get to challenge an opponent and win, claiming glory until the next match. It is a symbolic war in which no one dies – crushed egos perhaps, but no one dies. Maybe sport is how we should settle our differences instead of war.

The game against France was a full house. Having colonised Lebanon, the French had left many things behind, including their language. Most Lebanese speak French as it is still taught in most schools instead of English. So was there politics involved in this arena? I thought so, fans cheered when the Lebanese–Aussies knocked the French out of the competition.

The journey to Lebanon filled me with emotions. Once my excitement began to settle I started to see the reality of a country trying to move on from its brutal, turbulent recent past. I saw buildings bearing the scars of warfare, with craters in their sides but somehow still standing. Bullet holes painfully decorated the walls of churches and mosques, schools and shops, and were a harsh reminder to everyone that nothing was off limits to the violence. The effects of war were all around.

Thinking about how it must have been – how the everyday struggle to feed a family was a reality for most – made me want to weep. The war had destroyed the Lebanese economy in ways only measurable in decades. The lack of jobs and destroyed industries, along with limited government funding, meant university graduates often had to look outside their profession for employment. One morning I went with Hazem to buy some cucumbers from the street vendor I'd heard and when I met him I could see his hands and face didn't look like those of a farmer who had worked on the land for years. His face looked as though he had had a hard life but not by the elements and being weathered by the sun. I was curious so I asked him whether he had been farming long and he said, 'I'm a pharmacist by profession but there is no work for me, so I sell vegetables just to pay the bills.' His father had worked hard to give his son a chance to be educated and the chance at a better life with a university degree, but it seemed that his father's efforts were in vain.

I asked him why that was and his answer horrified me. He told me only about one in fifty people could afford medicine and so if there were no customers for a pharmacy then there was no work. The man with the cucumbers was no longer the nostalgic sound of a romantic homeland memory, he was now the bearer of a horrifying truth and reality. What we took for granted in

Australia, from safety to electricity and everything in between, was a luxury here not available to many.

I found myself wanting to fix everything, but of course I couldn't. No matter how much we gave it was a drop in an ocean needing so much more. As the trip came to an end I was starting to get homesick, I missed Sydney so much. When I finally flew home I had changed and grown. The problems I saw in Hazem's homeland altered my, until then, romantic image of the Middle East. I have to believe we can fix what's wrong with the world, from disease and hunger to poverty, oppression and homelessness; but standing in the way are corrupt greedy tyrant leaders with a lack of sensitivity to their fellow human beings. The current revolution that has occurred in the Middle East has happened because people's natural need for freedom and justice can't be stifled and people want to see change for the better.

It was a long flight and when we finally got to Sydney we circled in the air for twenty minutes before we landed. It was a beautiful sunny Sydney morning and I looked out the window of the plane to see the sunshine hitting the water in the harbour. It was almost blinding, but I wanted to see the Opera House standing tall, the Harbour Bridge streaming with cars full of my fellow countrymen heading out to work, and the grey-blue haze of gum trees in the bush on the outskirts of the city. I started to cry, burying my face in Hazem's warm chest. He didn't ask me why; he knew . . . I was home.

Khubz Arabi (Arab bread)

Ingredients

- 2½ cups warm water
- 2 packages active dry yeast
- 1 tablespoon salt
- ½ tsp sugar (optional)
- 6 cups all-purpose flour, sifted
- 2 tablespoons vegetable oil

Method

In a large bowl, scatter the yeast over the warm water and stir until dissolved. Add the salt and sugar. While kneading constantly, gradually add 6 cups of flour and 2 tablespoons of oil until the dough is smooth and elastic. Continue to add more flour if the dough still sticks to your hands.

Put the dough into a large, greased bowl and turn dough to grease all sides. Cover with a dry tea towel and let rise in a warm place until doubled in size. This should take about 1½ hours.

Preheat oven to 190°C. Punch dough down gently. Divide the dough into 24 equal portions and shape them each into smooth balls. Place on a floured surface and dust tops lightly with flour. Cover with a dry tea towel. Let rest undisturbed 15 minutes more.

Roll out each ball into a 6-inch diameter circle. Place on greased baking sheets. Bake in 190°C oven for 10–12 minutes or until the bread puffs. Do not leave baking unattended.

Makes 24 pieces.

Chapter Thirteen

A Football Wife

My family is the most important focus of my life and I was happy to put all my efforts into my children and Hazem's career once I finished university. But neither of us realised that Hazem's career would take us on such a rollercoaster of emotions. It would bring us tremendous joy, and test our strength, and would also bring us a heavy sadness. Hazem's beloved Bulldogs were more than a team to him: it was the community that he had been part of since he was a teenager and he could never have anticipated the scandals that were to come. From salary cap scandals to dismissed CEOs and misbehaving players – all became front-page fodder and fuel for gossip. Hazem's career withstood it all and he was one of the players who supported the club no matter what. I am so proud of him and he stands tall among the club's legends. He broke nearly every single record at the Bulldogs, along with some long-standing NRL records that had been considered unbreakable for many years. With his consistency, dedication and loyalty he obliterated most of them. He is one of only a handful of players to have played over three hundred games at the same club and his farewell match was a day we will treasure forever.

We got through it all, good times and bad, but the hardest thing Hazem and I ever had to deal with was when the Bulldogs were caught up in a rape scandal. The team was away at a pre-season trial match at Coffs Harbour on the New South Wales mid-north coast when a young woman reported she had been raped by a number of Canterbury Bulldogs players. The allegations soon hit the media and it was difficult to separate fact from gossip as television, radio and newspapers speculated wildly, and appeared not to worry whether they were reporting facts or fiction. No one knew who was alleged to have been involved and so all the players were tainted, including Hazem.

I trust my husband completely, I know him and never, ever for one moment would he be in any situation where he is compromised in any way. He is an honourable man and true to his faith and to me. And yet I had people I barely knew questioning me about Hazem's fidelity. At one point the whole team was asked to take a DNA test and Hazem refused. He was not involved, he was not accused, he had done nothing wrong and yet he was being treated like he was a criminal. The hysteria his decision caused was upsetting for all of us; he was a respected guy with no track record of any bad behaviour in anything, but all that didn't matter. People kept saying, 'Well, if he has nothing to hide, why doesn't he just take the test?' Talkback radio was buzzing with people attacking him. I listened as commentators and callers dissected my husband and me, our personal life and especially my intimacy with Hazem. It was devastating and demoralising. It seemed the public fury had no boundaries and everyone was free to comment on and judge the issues. For Hazem it was a matter of principle. To have submitted his DNA in a matter so demeaning to satisfy people's doubts was not acceptable and I supported him all the way.

A Football Wife

As Hazem was fighting the wave of criticism in the media, I had to face people in my everyday life. I was at the local shopping centre buying some fresh yoghurt and chatting to the woman in the shop. We'd talked many times before. She knew me and she knew Hazem and yet she had no hesitation in asking 'Is your husband involved? He's not one of them, is he?' I was horrified that even people who knew us still had doubts. I wasn't going to explain anything to anyone; I held my tears in and left the shop quickly. That night I cried as I told Hazem what had happened. I wasn't the only football wife who had to deal with the same public questioning and suspicious eyes. No matter what we said in defence of our innocent partners or husbands, people had made up their own minds that they were all guilty. My dear friend Jo Price told me how her husband Steven took the DNA test, even though he wasn't a suspect and she wished he hadn't done so. Even after that the suspicious looks never stopped.

Eventually the Director of Public Prosecutions announced that there was insufficient evidence to take the case further. It wasn't the definitive statement of innocence we wanted to hear but it took the focus off the players. That moment would pass but not its pain. For me it showed that in public life, even if you have done nothing wrong, nothing is off limits. The stress of that time didn't affect our relationship, it made it stronger and we matured as a couple. The love and support that we give each other every day is what is important.

Hazem played and won his first and only grand final with the Bulldogs in 2004. That moment in his career is one filled with happiness and relief at the same time. I was glad he had achieved that all-important milestone in his career, not one that all players get to share. It's right up there with Hazem's selection to play for Australia and represent his country on the football field. For me the proudest moment in Hazem's career as a football player was when he was selected to play for the New South Wales Blues in the third game of the State of Origin series.

Hazem came home buzzing with the news he'd been selected to play for New South Wales in the upcoming game at Brisbane's famous Suncorp stadium. The Queenslanders are known for their passion for football and the State of Origin brings out the best in the Maroons' supporters. I was extremely happy for Hazem as were both our families. I travelled with his brothers and mine to watch him play. It was the first time I had travelled to Brisbane and when we arrived at the stadium I was the only veiled Muslim woman in the crowd. Everyone recognised who I was. People passed by wearing their Queensland jerseys and they'd stop and say, 'It's good he finally got picked to play. It's gonna be good to watch him tonight, you must be so proud!' I was so happy to hear such honest and human words from a rival opposition that most of the time despises anything about the Blues.

As I watched Hazem take the field I could see only a few scattered Blues' supporters in a sea of Maroon. It was basically a dead rubber because Queensland had won the first two games in the best of three series, but I didn't see it that way. As far as I was concerned it was Hazem's time to shine in the Blues jersey he'd always deserved.

As the match started we were sitting right under an open members' box filled with diehard Queenslanders. They looked down at us and watched us cheer every time Hazem touched the ball. When Hazem lined up his first kick I prayed for him to get it; it was right on the sideline so wasn't an easy shot. The supporters in the box yelled out, 'We hope he gets it in.' I held my breath as he took a few steps, swung his boot and kicked that ball in front of fifty thousand diehard Maroons' supporters booing him; he looked up as it just floated between the uprights. I jumped up in a cheer and saw many Queensland supporters cheering with me. It wasn't bad for the oldest debutant in Blues' history. The guys in the box called down and said, 'He's a great player, you must be proud.' I was, we all were. The Blues won the game and we celebrated together. We walked down the main street of Brisbane and Maroon supporters kept stopping Hazem to shake his hand and have a photo taken with him. They loved him and it meant a lot getting that sort of attention from rival fans.

We travelled back to Sydney and, as I was putting his playing gear in the washing machine, I opened up his bag and was hit by the smell of the earth and freshly cut grass. Normally I don't get to wash Hazem's jersey as it's washed by the club, but he'd got to keep his Origin jersey and he had stuffed it into his bag as soon as he took it off. I picked it up and saw all the grass marks and soil stains, the evidence of the fearsome battle that had take place. I lifted it up to my face and smelled it again, and it was as though I was on the field with him. For the first time in his football career I felt so close to the action and what he does out there on the field. The whole experience of being in Brisbane and watching him play had finally sunk in. It had taken a long time but finally it wasn't a dream, it was a reality.

I was so pleased that when Hazem ended his career he received the recognition he deserved. But life after football was not the easy transition that everyone had imagined. The Bulldogs were initially unable to find any role for Hazem when he retired from playing and we found ourselves in uncharted waters. It was an extremely difficult time and it tested our relationship.

But Hazem is not alone in experiencing such struggles. Many players who retire from this great game end up having difficulties. Unlike a trade or qualification, sport is based on the physical ability you possess while you are still youthful and able to deliver. The NRL has many initiatives to prepare players for their life after football, but on a club level the success rate for this is not very high. The reality is that these players are the forgotten heroes who brought us immense joy when they played in our teams – we cheer for them and cry with them – yet when they give it all up they are mostly forgotten.

Only a select few manage to stay linked professionally to the game and to my eye they are not always the ones with an unblemished and decorated career with high achievements; they are sometimes quite the opposite. And yet with that public role they become the face of a game that I believe deserves a better image than that. It's all quite extraordinary. We all assume athletes are set for life and don't need to work, but this isn't the case. Of course they are paid well when they are playing, but a young man retiring from a job at thirty-three years of age still has more than half his life ahead of him and has to pay the bills. If a player is wise they will invest their money well to prepare for the end of their footy life. But the reality often is that these young men, who look grown up physically, are still young teenagers and they are vulnerable. When they make mistakes they are usually very costly ones. Certain people see them as easy prey; they promise them the world and they end up with nothing. Hazem was one of the young men who trusted those he shouldn't have – he fell victim to bad advice. It is a common experience shared by people with a newly found fortune. They were hard lessons to learn, but Hazem and I now know who we can trust.

I regard it as a privilege that I have been able to meet and get to know people in the family of rugby league that otherwise I never would have known. It has been an enriching experience to say the least. I have had the pleasure of introducing them to our life through the power of food. I have hosted so many dinners with friends who have never eaten Arab food, some who have never spoken to a Muslim person before. With the age-old ritual of eating together, breaking bread together, we were able to share some of ourselves with someone else. In fact the idea of writing this book came about during a dinner with friends. While enjoying my food, they suggested I write a book.

I made many friends through the family of football who I love dearly and I have watched them struggle even more than we did with life after football. These young families find the shift from a high-profile life into a normal life difficult to make, and quite often the tension spells the end of the relationship. I have met many women previously married to athletes who have all said the same thing: 'It's different after he gave it all up.' There is no security, no safety blanket and no preparation.

Hazem and I weren't an exception to this tension, as it touched us too. I thought we were strong enough to handle this huge shift, but the reality is that no matter how smart you think you are, you can never be prepared for everything. I found life different when Hazem suddenly became available after a decade of always being too busy. He has always been actively involved in family life and especially with the children, but he went missing many times due to his professional commitments. Women in these relationships always have to fill that gap, and that's what I happily did. I made sure he had the time and space to prepare for a game and cooked the pasta and rice dishes he needed the days before. But I also filled the gap when he travelled and wasn't there. To have him suddenly become permanently available was something we had to get used to. It was as though we had to rediscover each other in some ways. We clashed a lot in the first few months of his retirement, but we never loved each other any less. We eventually settled into the normal lifestyle we always wished for and that experience eventually made us even stronger. But tragically not all make it to the other side.

Reem's creamy chicken and mushroom pasta

Ingredients

- 600ml fresh cream
- 1 tsp salt
- 2 garlic cloves, crushed
- Fresh cracked black pepper
- 2 tsp flour
- 2 cups fresh mushrooms, sliced
- 250g cooked chicken, chopped
- 1 tsp dried oregano leaves
- 250g fettuccine or penne pasta, cooked
- A handful of chopped flat-leaf parsley

Method

In a pan place the cream, salt, garlic, pepper and flour and whisk until it thickens. Add the fresh mushrooms and chicken and oregano. Allow it come to the boil and then toss in the cooked pasta and chopped parsley. Mix well and serve with herb bread.

Serves 4 to 6 people.

Chapter Fourteen

Where the Heart is . . .

In Arab tradition, when the first son enters this world the parents are called by their firstborn son's name. With the birth of Zayd, Hazem was *Abou Zayd* (father of Zayd) and I was now *Um Zayd* (mother of Zayd). Hazem and I had chosen Zayd's name even before we knew he was a boy, but his pregnancy was so different to Lamya's that I was certain he was going to be a boy. That maternal instinct I mentioned earlier kicked in. But I did worry that I was wrong . . . like my mother was when she was pregnant with me!

Hazem and I always wanted our children to have names that were linked to our Arab heritage but we also wanted the Australian tongue to pronounce them with ease. We wanted our children to have names that were the same in English as they were in Arabic. Many letters in the Arabic alphabet don't translate to English very well because some are throaty and lose their beauty when replaced. Lamya's name is a word used in Arabic poetry that describes the beautiful soft lips of a woman; Zayd's name means 'plentiful' and is also the name of one of Prophet Mohammad's companions. Our third child Serene's name means the same in English and Arabic, tranquil and peaceful. It's also the name of a small town in Palestine. There is much pride and love in both our hearts as parents when we see how our children have grown. We sit back and watch them play and learn from us, not just from Hazem and me but from the whole family: their grandparents, uncles and aunts. In my opinion it's not only a mother and father who raise a child but the whole family unit that supports, loves and teaches the next generation of our family. All working together collectively and, to a large extent, unconsciously. Lamya has become a bright and keen cook, always helping me in the kitchen with anything I make. She grabs her baker's kit and rolls up her sleeves, ready to measure up. I'm so happy when she asks me, 'Mum are we making *mamoul* this year for *Eid*?' I know that some of me is now within her too.

Zayd is always an unwilling participant in cooking, but rushes over to lick the bowl after Lamya and Serene help me whip up a chocolate cake. Zayd has inherited Hazem's competitive nature. His energy to stay on the field for the whole soccer match is wonderful to watch. Being the children of a sporting father, it is only fitting to have both Lamya and Zayd on the same soccer team. Lamya, being the only girl on a team of boys, was reluctant to join but as the goalkeeper she handles it well. As Zayd grows and pays closer attention to all the invaluable tips Hazem yells out to him from the sideline he is proving to us that he might just follow in his father's footsteps. I watch him improve and have fun as he kicks the ball and lands a goal, he looks over at his dad and me and give us the thumbs up. Serene jumps up in a cheer and unbelievably remembers the score! Serene is one of those children who will give nearly everything a go and get it right. She is an observant child who became self-sufficient quite quickly. Such an easy personality, our time with her alone while Lamya and Zayd are at school has made our relationship with her closer, even though she is the youngest. Serene shares Hazem's sense of humour and my love of books. All three children are big readers as they sit and listen to me read to them a story in both English and Arabic. Lamya and Zayd are learning both English and Arabic at school and read, write and recite the Quran in Arabic quite well. This privilege of languages helps connect them to both worlds. I am grateful for being able to be with my children during the most important years of their lives, to care for them and teach them through that invaluable role of mother that I am privileged to have known.

And it wasn't only me who felt it. The rest of our family began to grow too. My sister Reem was pregnant around the same time I was with both Zayd and Serene. Reem and Akheel moved to the Central Coast early in their married life. Reem was a teacher and he was an engineer, both working in their professions during the day, and at night they ran an Italian pizza and pasta restaurant that was loved by the locals. I was so happy when my sister moved back to Sydney when she was pregnant with her daughter Sophia. This Palestinian–Australian couple bought an Italian restaurant and they both cook there. Another example of Australian multiculturalism at work. After their move and the births of Sophia and son Joseph, Reem and Akheel would experience a devastating blow that many people around the world have gone through. In late 2009 Akheel was diagnosed with leukaemia. This experience devastated both their families. You never think it will happen to you but when someone in your family is affected you know that these illnesses are blind to race or religion or creed. During the time of Akheel's treatment, Reem and I grew even closer as we all helped them through it. Akheel is today in remission and on the road to recovery, Allah willing. My heart goes out to anyone who lives with an illness like cancer, as life as you know it changes in the blink of an eye.

The early years of motherhood put me through some tough times. The learning curve of trial and error was something I felt mostly with Zayd. Zayd was born on 2 July 2004. From the moment he was born Zayd needed more attention than Lamya had, he was a crying baby and even when he was older he went through a tantrum stage that put a lot of stress on me. I found myself housebound many times as it was so difficult to go out, even to the shops for milk and bread, without Zayd screaming the whole trip. He just wanted to be at home with his mum all the time. In those early years, if I needed to take a shower Hazem would hold him while he screamed for the whole fifteen minutes. It was a difficult time for both of us and it kept me away from the football and watching Hazem play many times. Zayd will hate reading this and he is long past the restless baby and toddler tantrum stages and has grown into a sensitive and concerned son. His love for his mum just got bigger as he got older and I feel blessed.

Hazem and I decided to perform the Hajj, the Islamic pilgrimage to Mecca, and we planned to leave Lamya with Hazem's parents and Zayd with my mum for the three weeks we would be away. I was so concerned about leaving Zayd that for a while I didn't think I should go. He was only two and a half years old and he was so attached to me I was worried both he and my mum wouldn't cope. I eventually decided it was an opportunity I couldn't turn down and thankfully Zayd was fine. He didn't even miss us; Mum took great care of him as did Hazem's parents of Lamya.

Where the Heart is . . .

* * *

Our trip to Mecca was a spiritual journey to strengthen our *iman*. *Iman* in Islam means to believe in Allah and his angels and all his books and all his prophets. And to believe in the day of judgment and Allah's predestination of things good or bad.

For Hazem and me to complete the final pillar of Islam was extremely important. The five pillars of Islam are very straightforward. The first is to believe in only one God, Allah, and that Mohammad is Allah's last messenger (*shahada*). The second pillar is to perform the five daily prayers (*salat*); the third is to fast (*sawm*); the fourth, to give charity (*zakat*), is the system of charity that deals with solving the situation of the uneven distribution of wealth in society. It allows the wealthy to stay rich but also looks after the less fortunate. It is a religious obligation not a choice. To look after the people in our society who are in need is a humanitarian duty regardless of faith or race. It replenishes your soul and to many is a natural high. Islam teaches that if you are a person who has some goodness to give, be it money or otherwise, it doesn't matter who is on the receiving end, Muslim or otherwise. In fact, Muslims are encouraged to give to all the needy, especially those who are not Muslims, as empathy and kindness supersedes any differences. This life rule I use in my everyday teachings to my children, our humanity should always prevail . . .

The fifth and final pillar is to make a pilgrimage to Mecca once in a lifetime (Hajj) if you are able to physically and financially during the pilgrimage season. Performing Hajj was the only pillar we hadn't achieved. I had performed *Umrah*, the visit to Mecca outside the holy month. When a Muslim returns from Hajj it is as though they are reborn and, with Allah's mercy and forgiveness, their sins are wiped away. We were always keen to go and talked about it many times but Hajj season always clashed with Hazem's football commitments. The 2006–07 Hajj season was when Hazem had his summer break so the time was right.

We booked our tickets and packed our bags; Muslims believe you don't choose to go to Hajj, you are chosen to go and that year it was our turn. I wanted to see the country I was born in one more time. I wanted to feel a physical connection to it. I wondered if it was going to be a feeling of coming home or not? And would it shake my newly found feeling of home in Australia? I wasn't sure; I had to wait and see.

We arrived in Saudi Arabia at an airport especially for pilgrims, just a few kilometres from Jeddah. Millions of people have come to perform the Hajj every year for over 1400 years, and in more recent times the Saudi Arabian government built an airport equipped to deal with these huge numbers. When we got off the airplane I took a deep breath and filled my lungs with the dry desert winter air, my heart was heavy as I remembered myself as a child back in Saudi Arabia. I could feel the desert around me as the waiting area was outdoors. It was night-time and I could hardly see anything but I could definitely feel it.

We sat down amongst thousands of travelling pilgrims from every country around the world. It was such an amazing sight: people from parts of the world I would never travel to all in the one place, all dressed in similar white pilgrim attire. But there was something strange that caught my eye; some of these people were carrying huge bags of onions, potatoes and other vegetables. I realised they were part of a big group of pilgrims who came from a poor country and they were carrying these staples to save on their expenses. I was concerned for them as I was sure the customs

Where the Heart is . . .

officers would confiscate their food as they do in Australia. To my surprise they didn't, they were all allowed through.

I was mystified and couldn't believe the Saudi government would overlook such an obvious danger to its country that only increases every year. When I returned to Sydney I researched this strange occurrence and found the explanation. Saudi Arabia is a desert landscape and nothing anyone will bring to its land can grow and destroy its ecosystem. How perfect the holy city of Mecca is in a land that seems so harsh and dry, but it is this that serves as a protection and enables visitors to be welcomed without restriction. It would have been impossible to search every passenger coming to Mecca for food, millions of people would need to be checked for food in a matter of a few days, which would have been a very difficult task.

While we were waiting, Hazem and I became hungry but in that part of the airport there were no shops to buy food. I had a special batch of Hindiya's date-filled *mamoul* with me and we ate that. Dates are a complete food source for travellers as their nutritional value is equivalent to a whole meal. *Mamoul* was the perfect meal for a traveller in the desert as it keeps well and there was plenty of it in Saudi Arabia. Dates are mentioned in the Quran and especially in the verse that communicates to Maryam (the Virgin Mary) as she was giving birth to Issa (Jesus). The angel Gabriel communicated to her to shake the branch of the palm tree she was sitting under and the dates would fall, and to eat them as they would give her strength.

As the day began to break the horizon of the endless sand was in front of me. I waited quietly with Hazem to board the plane to Medina, the city where Prophet Mohammad is buried. I held the bars of the fence that surrounded the airport and looked out onto the landscape my heart had longed to see again for so many years. The fine powder-like sand that I remembered was everywhere I looked. A small breeze whipped up and suddenly it was all over my shoes. I knelt down and touched it but it wasn't enough. I wanted to walk in the desert with my bare feet and rub my hands in the sand. The fence stopped me and then it was time to board the plane for Medina, which was only an hour or so away.

As soon as we landed in Medina we were greeted by our guide and we joined our group of Muslim Aussie pilgrims who had headed out of Sydney a week ahead of us. It was like stepping into another dimension, walking the earth that the prophet had walked 1400 years ago. The desert air was somehow perfumed, the earth was calm as if my senses were still and allowed my inner heart to awake. I couldn't wait to see Prophet Mohammad's resting place.

Our hotel was right across the road from Al-Masjid al-Nabawi (the mosque of Prophet Mohammad). The mosque is special for many reasons – the original structure was built by Prophet Mohammad himself, a small back room was his home and ultimately his burial site. The tomb of the prophet is covered by an immense green dome that is one of the most beloved architectural marvels of the Muslim world.

We walked through the main reception area in the hotel and it was filled with people from all nationalities who were all in similar clothes, you couldn't tell where they were from. But it didn't take long to work out who the Muslim Aussies were as they recognised Hazem right away. We made our way to our rooms and I looked out the window for the first time and saw the grand size of the mosque. The prophet is laid to rest there, beside him lay his two most loyal companions, Abu Bakr and Omar. Prophet Mohammad died resting his head on his wife Aisha's lap. One of the last words communicated by the prophet to mankind was to be kind to women as they are your equals.

Aisha as a woman in Islam has played a significant role in narrating the teachings that the prophet communicated to her, amongst many were issues especially about women for women, and thereby removing any element of embarrassment. Women, contrary to what most think, played a pivotal part in Islam's survival and continuance now and in history. Aisha communicated the largest part of Prophet Mohammad's authentic teachings.

I placed my things in my room and headed straight to the mosque with Hazem to pray and have a look around, but as soon as we were in the lobby of the hotel we were swamped with fellow Australians who came to talk to Hazem, happy at his presence. I looked at him from a distance and realised that for the whole trip he would be forever in the company of others. My spiritual journey with my husband turned into a continuous search for a moment to be by ourselves. I wasn't going to let it bother me and I removed myself from that and left Hazem to be in demand as he always is. I felt sorry for him as he wasn't there representing the Bulldogs, but no matter where we were if there were footy-loving Australians around he was going to be recognised. That's something we had to deal with even in the heart of Saudi Arabia.

I spent so much time in the holy mosque of Medina as I sat and prayed and waited for the following prayer to be called. I stood side by side with millions in a mosque that is so grand and beautiful; Africans and Chinese, Indians and Europeans, all in their colourfully different attire. I sat for hours reciting the holy Quran. I would spend time looking at people's faces and try and guess their nationalities and I tried to talk to as many people as I could, learning where they were from. They all had such interesting faces and came from all over the world.

I sat and asked Allah for guidance and direction in my life, for peace and strength to always do the right thing. I prayed for peace on earth to all mankind and to help me raise good children to be good people and good Muslims.

I visited the prophet's home and prayed in his presence. I said '*Assalamu allaikum*' to him and his companions. I walked out on to the streets of Medina and visited the cemetery al-Baqi where many of the people I learned of in Islamic history were buried, along with the prophet's companions and the prophet's wife Aisha.

It was a desert cemetery and there were hundreds of birds flying above and roosting on the graves. I prayed for all these people who had helped me learn about my religion. I spent a lot of time by myself thinking, praying, but I also went to the shops and bought dates that were in so many different varieties and all equally delicious. I bought clothes and perfumes, I visited bookshops in search of some historical books to bring home to my library, I found the most amazing book that had images of Islamic artefacts and bought it right away.

When I returned I spotted Hazem in the hotel lobby still surrounded by people. He came up to me and apologised for being away from me but I knew it wasn't his fault and I told him so. We were in a lift going up to our room when a man got into the lift and said '*Assalamu alaikum*', peace be upon you, in proper Islamic greeting with perfect Arabic pronunciation. He was dressed in a traditional Saudi Arabian men's outfit but he was as blond as some of my girlfriends in Australia, with fair freckled skin. We both smiled and asked him, 'Where are you from, brother?' He said, 'I'm from England.' He told us he was born and bred British and had found peace in Islam more than twenty years before. At that moment I had hope that Islam is truly universal and is not only for people who are Arab, it's for anyone. I couldn't contain myself and smiled widely; he smiled back at us and said, 'Is that an Aussie accent I hear?' Hazem and I both said at the same time, 'Yes, we're Australian, from Sydney.'

I paused for a second and realised how easy that was. For both of us to announce that we were Australian, without any hesitation, it rolled off our tongues with pride. In the heart of Medina, where my faith felt at home, I knew I was Muslim but I was also Australian. I realised my heart knew it before my mind did. But I was still concerned. Would it be the same when I was in Mecca or when I saw Dad's family in Jeddah? . . . I would have to wait and see.

A few days later it was time to farewell Prophet Mohammad's tomb and mosque and make our way to the holy city Mina to begin our pilgrimage. It was bustling, full of people and markets that sold essential things.

By then Hazem and I still had so few moments alone, I was starting to get frustrated by it and we ended up having an argument before we began our Hajj. When we arrived in Arafat, Hazem called out to me from outside the women's tent, 'Bring your things and hurry!' He wanted to make sure we had some time together so he whisked me away and found a small, private spot on the mountain, or as private as it could be amongst a few million people. On the mountain of Arafat I prayed to Allah and opened my heart to him as I stood shoulder to shoulder with Hazem. I felt so close to Hazem, up until then we had not been alone together in prayer. It was a very special time. I looked at the sky and watched the colours change as evening came and the sun started to set. I stared at the endless night sky and prayed for so many things. I prayed for peace and forgiveness for all mankind.

It is well known to all Muslims that if you ask Allah for anything on the mountain of Arafat in Hajj it shall be granted and I had hoped to see it in my lifetime. Standing there, Hazem and I were following the Sunna of Prophet Mohammad, this Sunna that had survived hundreds of years.

The next morning we were all told to get ready to go to Mecca for the final part of our Hajj. Finally, I was going to see the magnificent Kaaba that I had visited as a child with my parents.

That visit to Mecca when I was a child had strengthened my love for the holy city, a love which had grown in my heart for eighteen years, and I was finally going to see it again. It was the same place but I was now a different person. I couldn't contain my happiness and felt so alive. The rest of the group we were travelling with took the bus but Hazem and I, along with a friend who lived in Saudi Arabia, decided to travel on foot the whole way to Mecca. It was about ten kilometres. It is said that when you enter Mecca on foot it is a much more stimulating experience of the Haram and takes you to the heart of the city. We walked to the casting of the stones then continued to Mecca. We walked in a tunnel built by the Saudi Arabian government that runs under the rest of the town. It was huge and was filled with a wave of people all heading in the same direction. I had an anxious feeling that lasted the whole walk; I think I was slightly overwhelmed by it all.

Finally we were at the end of the tunnel and I took a deep breath as the structure of the Haram began to take shape in my eyes. It was grand and in a sort of valley, all the surrounding buildings were on higher ground. I was in awe of this place and its people, things are different in the eyes of a child but now I was an adult and I could see it all. It looked different, with so many extensions and developments to cater for the millions who travelled there each year. The Haram is currently undergoing a new renovation to further expand its capacity. The renovation began in 2007 and is due to finish in 2020. The manpower used to assist the pilgrims and accommodation for them alone is beyond explanation.

There were waves of people as far as my eye could see all heading in the same direction. Imagine yourself amongst eighty thousand fans leaving the Olympic stadium after a footy match at the same time, heading in the same direction and multiply that by forty. The sensation is surreal. Everyone was heading peacefully in a natural flow gravitating to the same place. I learned that if Hajj teaches a person anything it definitely teaches patience. To be sharing such an experience and place with a few million people who don't all speak the same language meant we had to read each other's body language and be patient and serene with one another.

In Mecca, along with the pilgrims, there is a large number of working-class migrants who flock there for the busiest and most profitable time of year. It was like the times of Prophet Mohammad when Mecca was the grand marketplace of the Arabian desert.

We walked around to one of the entrances; Hazem grabbed my hand in the avalanche of people around us, trying to guide me through. Finally we were there. I saw it! But at first I wasn't sure. Right in front of me the Kaaba looked new. This building that is as old as the Prophet Ibrahim looked as if it was a fibreglass shell. I knew it was there to protect its original structure with only one original outer wall exposed. That was enough.

I stood there for hours, just staring at it and praying to Allah. I began to notice the birds flying above the Kaaba in a systematic rotation, singing the most beautiful songs over and over. I was mesmerised but puzzled. With a hundred or so birds above I could see not even one sign of bird droppings anywhere. Not on the walls where they rested or the floor where we walked barefoot, not even on the revealing black cover of the Kaaba. These birds are known to pilgrims as the birds of the Haram, they are there all day and night. I found it amazing, could these birds know that this is a holy place and do their business elsewhere? That was the only explanation that fit; Muslims believe that animals and plants all worship Allah in their own way, maybe these birds were on a pilgrimage just like me.

I turned and faced the wave of people walking around the Kaaba, performing Tawaf, which means walking around the Kaaba seven times. I could see their differences and similarities: the way they dressed and looked, the colour of their skin and their race. Watching all those people was too overwhelming so I sat down and began to look at their feet. There are so many things you can learn about a person by looking at their feet, without even seeing their face.

I was thirsty from the walk and Hazem and I found one of the many taps in the Haram. I took a drink and that unmistakable taste of Zamzam water I once had as a child was instantly recognisable. I drank as much as I could before Hazem and I started our own Tawaf around the Kaaba. We made our way to the top level of the mosque and began to circle seven times counter clockwise with the Kaaba to our left while chanting '*Labbaik Allahumma labbaik . . .*' which means 'I am totally at your service, o Allah'; along with a few million people. After that we walked seven times between Safa and Marwah, as Hagar did when looking for water in the desert with her young son, Ismail, son of Ibrahim.

My feet were so sore I wanted to sit and rest, but every time I drank Zamzam water a new strength would help me keep going. When we were done Hazem had to get his hair shaved and I had to have a small snip taken of my hair; this is the final act of purification and marks the completion of the major part of Hajj.

Where the Heart is . . .

While waiting for Hazem to be done, I noticed how every man wearing the Hajj outfit looked identical, no one was better than anyone else. You couldn't tell who was rich and who was poor, who was sick and who was not; they all looked the same, they had all shed their worldly possessions and were seeking Allah's forgiveness and mercy. It was a sight that made all the hair on my body stand up.

My father was in Saudi Arabia visiting his family while we were there so the next day we called him from the hotel and he came to pick us up to take us to visit his family in Jeddah. We were only allowed out of Mecca for forty-eight hours as our visa was only for Hajj so it was going to be a quick stay. Dad arrived with one of my uncles and I ran to him and hugged him so tight as I hadn't seen him for years. On the hour's drive we talked the whole way and when I got to his home I met my cousins for the first time. My grandmother Amira was there too, as soon as I laid eyes on her I cried and kissed her hands. She was in a wheelchair after a stroke that left her weak and with massive memory loss. She didn't even remember my dad's name. It saddened me greatly to see her in that way, in my memory she was laughing in the company of our whole family enjoying the *Mansaf* she had cooked the last time we visited her before heading out to Australia. None of us knew then it would be eighteen years before we would again be together. After spending time catching up, my aunt came to pick us up and we went to see my grandfather Omar who was staying at her home. Unlike Amira, my grandfather remembered me. He was in much better health. I kissed his hand and sat beside him and told him about Australia and his great-grandchildren.

I showed him photos of our children as I looked over at my father and realised for the first time how much he resembled his dad. We spent the night at my aunt's house and all my uncles, aunts and cousins came over for lunch the next day. We sat and talked, eating huge plates of *kabsa* and different salads, laughing and remembering old times. At that moment I realised that my children would never feel this distance with their immediate family as we were all together in the same place and I felt blessed and thankful. Too quickly it was time to go and I left not knowing if we were ever going to meet again.

Sadly it would be the last time I saw Amira and Omar. Amira passed away in 2007 and not long after Omar passed away too. My father was back in Australia at the time and he was deeply saddened for weeks at his parents' passing and the fact that he couldn't be with his family to mourn their deaths. A few weeks later Dad received a large envelope in the post, and when he opened it he began to cry. It was his share of his father's inheritance, but this wasn't an ordinary inheritance, it was copies of old documents stamped with the government of Palestine and the British Coat of Arms. These were the land deeds my great-grandfather and grandfather owned back in the old country, Palestine. When my father reminisced about how his family used to own half the town it turned out he wasn't exaggerating; the deeds totalled up to 4,000,000 square metres of farm land and property. They were kings in their home who woke up one day refugees with nothing. My father inherited his father's pain of losing what was his because of the Israeli invasion.

As he held those deeds, Dad told me how his grandfather had died from depression as the wait to go home to Palestine went on so long. I knew one day it would be the turn of me and my brothers and sisters to inherit Dad's grief for what has been lost in the old

Where the Heart is . . .

country. Although I have never seen it, my heart longs to walk the streets of Jerusalem in peace, to breathe its air and eat its olives and rub my hands in its earth. To run in the orchards my father has told me he used to play in as a child, picking the oranges from the trees. As long as I live I will carry some of my family's sadness and loss. And yet, that burden is much easier to bear knowing I now have a home of my own, a place of safety and love.

Mecca is a city that doesn't sleep during Hajj, everything is open all hours of the day, except when it is time for prayer, then the shops close and people head out to pray. During the five calls to prayer pilgrims fill the Haram and pour out onto the sidewalks, spread their prayer mats and join the imam in *salat* (prayer).

After some last-minute gift shopping for family and friends, Hazem and I said our final goodbyes to the holy city of Mecca in a final Tawaf around the Kaaba. My eyes were full of tears, not because I wanted to stay but because I realised my heart was ready to go home and that I was going to miss it. I prayed for Allah to give me the chance to return again with Hazem and our children so we could instil in them the love for Mecca that all Muslims share.

My journey home to the country I was born in was like the journey of Prophet Mohammad, who left his beloved Mecca in the times of hardship and danger after Islam was bestowed upon him. He took his followers and went to the safe place of Medina. The people of Medina welcomed him and made it a protected town for him, and many of them converted to Islam as they learned more from the prophet as the years went by. When Allah instructed the prophet to return to Mecca and perform the Hajj, the people of Medina were heavy-hearted, concerned he might want to stay once he arrived and that he might forget all about them. But he saw their concern and assured them no matter how much he missed Mecca and loved it he was returning back to Medina with them.

Just like me. I was going home exhausted and tired but I was going home. Mecca would always be in my heart; no matter where I was in the world. I realised my link to this beautiful place was a matter of faith. I will never forget my childhood memories, and the fact that most of my father's family still live there will always bring me back, but I will always return to where my heart is.

We returned to Sydney and, just like when we flew back from Lebanon, I had missed everything about it – the people, its crazy weather, beaches, its landscape and diversity, all of which, like my faith, are permanently a part of my being. It is what defines me as a proud Australian.

With my youngest brother Mohammad married we are all watching my parents grow old, happy to see us around them. We all realise our family has grown and, as my parents celebrate more grandchildren – Lamya, Zayd and Serene, along with Reem's children Sophia and Joseph, Maha with her firstborn son, Justice – we now know that we are here . . . here to stay.

Life has changed for Hazem and I now that he has finished playing football; some normality has found its way into our lives. No matter how normal it gets he will always be Hazem El Masri the football legend, but at home among his children he is Dad, legend of the pillow fight . . . as we watch our children grow the next chapter in our lives is only around the corner. Hazem is working in the community – a job that keeps him among the wider Australian community that he loves so much, doing what he has always done: being a positive role model.

Where the Heart is...

For me, this is the beginning of a dream of working in the community with women who share a passion to make a difference for all women.

With my home firmly in my heart, I am here with all that life has shown me. I was able to learn, grow and survive. The amazing women in my life who have enriched me and taught me how to be a strong woman will eternally be with me.

I am sitting here writing this after a wonderful afternoon in my home in Sydney's western suburbs. I am a happy Muslim Australian woman. I have been outside under the warm autumn sun with the breeze in my hair. My children ran around in the backyard and Hazem was fixing something in the back shed while I dug in my herb patch. Lamya got off her bike and came and sat beside me and asked, 'Mum, what's that?' She was pointing at the basil bush in the garden. 'That's basil *habibty*, the one mentioned in the Quran, in Arabic it's called *rihhan*.'

Lamya, in the way of children, had more questions. 'What do you use it for?' I told her I use it a lot in the sausage rolls she and her brother and sister love. 'Oh, yeah, the ones Tetah makes!' she said. I asked her to help me pick some, and also some rosemary for the lasagne I was going to make for dinner. Later, I could hear Hazem and our children talking in the lounge room as I stood in my Australian kitchen, cooking some Italian food and chopping up a Greek salad with Fayrouz singing softly in the background – it was a perfect end to a perfect Aussie afternoon. Now that I have found my home all I need to be happy is my faith, my family... and people I can feed.

Lamb shoulder and rice Ouzi-style

Ingredients for lamb shoulder

- 1½ kg lamb shoulder (bone in)
- 6 sprigs fresh rosemary
- Zest of 1 lemon
- 1 tsp salt
- 1 tsp ground cinnamon
- 1 tsp ground pimento
- 1 tsp ground black pepper
- ½ tsp ground nutmeg
- ¼ cup olive oil

Ingredients for rice

- 1 cup medium-grain rice
- 1 cup long-grain rice
- 750ml chicken stock
- ½ tsp salt
- ½ tsp ground cinnamon
- ½ tsp ground pimento
- ¼ tsp ground nutmeg
- 2 tsp butter

Ingredients for rice topping

- 1 tbs butter
- 1 brown onion, chopped
- 500g lean lamb medium mince
- ½ tsp salt
- ¼ tsp black pepper
- ¼ tsp ground pimento

¼ tsp ground cinnamon
1 cup slivered almonds
1 tbs butter for frying almonds

Method for lamb shoulder
Preheat oven to 200°C. Remove the rosemary leaves and chop them finely. Combine all the ingredients together in a bowl and mix well. Place lamb in a roasting tray and rub the mixture, massaging it into the meat, then secure the shoulder with strings. Place the lamb in the oven on a roasting dish and roast for 30 minutes. Reduce the heat to 160°C and turn the lamb fat side down and roast for one hour. Turn the lamb again and roast for another hour or until lamb melts off the bone when pulled away. Allow to rest for a few minutes before cutting.

Method for rice and mince topping
It is best to start cooking the rice 20 minutes before the lamb is ready to come out of the oven.

Soak the medium- and long-grain rice together for 15 minutes then drain well. In a pot bring the stock to the boil and add all the spices and butter. Pour in the rice then reduce the heat to low and cook for 15 to 20 minutes. When ready, remove from the heat, wrap pot with a towel and set aside until ready to serve.

Melt the butter in a frypan then add chopped onions and cook them until translucent without browning them. Add mince and cook through then add the spices and mix well.

In a separate frypan melt the butter and fry the almonds until golden brown, add to the mince and mix.

To serve it Arabian-style place the rice on a large serving dish and top with the mince and almond mix then place the lamb shoulder on the bed of rice. Enjoy with fresh cucumber and yoghurt salad.

Serves 4 to 6 people.

Samka Mashwi (oven-baked fish)

Ingredients

- 3 garlic cloves
- 1 medium piece of ginger, peeled and chopped
- 1 red chilli, de-seeded
- Zest of 1 lemon
- ½ cup extra virgin olive oil
- 1½ tsp salt
- ½ tsp black pepper
- ½ tsp dried chilli flakes
- 1 tsp sweet paprika
- 1 spring onion, finely chopped
- ½ cup coriander, chopped
- ½ cup flat-leaf parsley, chopped
- 1.5 to 2kg whole Snapper fish, cleaned
- Juice of 2 lemons
- 1 potato, peeled and sliced thinly (round slices)

Method

In a food processor finely chop the garlic and ginger with the chilli, making sure you don't puree them. Place them in a bowl and add the lemon zest, olive oil, salt, pepper, chilli, paprika, spring onion, coriander and parsley. Mix well.

Make three diagonal cuts on both sides of the fish and coat with the marinade, making sure you fill the cuts and cavity. Set a small amount of the marinade aside and add the lemon juice. Line the baking tray with the slices of potatoes and drizzle with a little olive oil. Place the fish on the bed of potatoes and cook in a hot oven (200°C) uncovered until skin slightly browns. The time may vary depending on the size of the fish.

Drizzle the fish with the remaining marinade as soon as it comes out of the oven.

Enjoy hot with an Arab tartar made from more finely chopped flat-leaf parsley in tahina, thinned with lemon juice and water, with a crushed clove of garlic and salt.

Serves 4 to 6 people.

Cucumber and yoghurt salad

Ingredients

- 1kg Greek-style yoghurt
- ½ cup water
- 1 tsp salt (or to taste)
- 1 tsp dried mint leaves
- 1 garlic clove (optional)
- 4 Lebanese cucumbers, diced finely

Method

Place the yoghurt in a bowl then add water, salt, garlic and mint. Mix well then add chopped cucumbers and mix. Serve cold with many rice dishes.

Serves 4 to 6 people.

Glossary

Al-Masjid al-Nabawi the mosque of the Prophet Mohammad, in Medina; home and burial site of the Prophet Mohammad
ashta Arab cream
Asr the mid-afternoon prayer
assalamu alaikum peace be with you
babaganoush Middle Eastern dish made from roasted and mashed eggplant
Bamia dish made with okra, lamb and tomato puree
Bayt Aisha the home of Aisha, wife of the Prophet Mohammad, within the Al-Masjid al-Nabawi
burqa traditional garment worn by Muslim women, giving full body covering with a narrow opening for the eyes
Dhuhr the midday prayer
Eid festival in the Islamic calendar
Eid-al-Fitr Eid festival after Ramadan, meaning 'the end of fast'
Fajr the time of the first prayers of the day; dawn
Fatiha, the opening chapter of the Quran

fatoush salad salad made with cucumbers, tomatoes and parsley with deep-fried flat bread and pomegranate dressing

foul dish of fava beans mashed with lemon juice, vinegar and tahina with olive oil and parsley

hadith teachings and stories from the life of the Prophet Mohammad; also a book (the Hadith)

Hajj pilgrimage to Mecca undertaken during the holy month; Fifth Pillar of Islam

Halal permissible under Islamic law

Haram site of the Masjid al-Haram, the Grand Mosque, in Mecca

hijab veil covering the hair, neck and chest, worn by Muslim women and girls who have reached puberty

Hijri calendar Islamic calendar that takes the year of the Prophet Mohammad's migration from Mecca to Medina as its starting point

hummus Middle Eastern dish made from cooked, mashed chickpeas, tahina, olive oil, lemon juice and garlic

imam a leader in prayer

Isha the fifth prayer of the day, an hour or so after sunset

Kaaba or Ka'aba an ancient stone cube-shaped structure in the centre of the Grand Mosque in Mecca; the centre of the Muslim world

kabsa Saudi dish made with rice, meat and vegetables and spiced with cardamom, cinnamon, bay leaves and curry

kanun Arabian stringed musical instrument

katayef sweet pancakes filled with ashta or chopped walnuts and sugared spices

khubz Arabi Arabic bread

kibbe pastry-encased meatballs made with lamb mince, pine nuts and pomegranate molasses

Glossary

kunafa traditional Middle Eastern sweet made from semolina, ashta, pistachio nuts and syrup

labbaik Allahumma labbaik translation: I am totally at your service, O Allah

labneh thickened yoghurt

Lahm bi Ajeen meat and vegetable pastries

Maghrib the fourth prayer of the day, at sunset

mahlab ground cherry kernel, used to flavour cakes, pastries and biscuits

mamoul traditional sweets filled with spiced dates, given out during Eid

Manoush traditional Arab pizza

Mansaf traditional Palestinian dish of lamb with yoghurt, onion, herbs and spices, rice, toasted almonds and pine nuts

Maramiah sage tea

Marwah one of two small mountains (the other is Safa) located in Mecca. Pilgrims ritually travel between Marwah and Safa seven times during the Hajj

Mecca city in Saudi Arabia; spiritual centre of Islam and birthplace of the Prophet Mohammad

Medina city in Saudi Arabia; burial site of the Prophet Mohammad

munazala dish made with mince-stuffed baby eggplants

oud Arabian stringed musical instrument, similar to a guitar

Qailulah Islamic rest period between midday and early afternoon

Quran the Holy Scripture of Islam

Quzi dish of roasted lamb and spices, stuffed with rice, mince and nuts

Ramadan the month of fasting and Hajj; holiest month of the Islamic calendar; the month when the message of Islam was bestowed upon the Prophet Mohammad

Safa one of two small mountains (the other is Marwah) located in Mecca. Pilgrims ritually travel between Marwah and Safa seven times during the Hajj

salat Second Pillar of Islam; to perform the five daily prayers

sambousek cheese- or meat-filled dough pastries

sawm Third Pillar of Islam; to fast

shahada First Pillar of Islam; that there is only one God, Allah, and that the Prophet Mohammad is Allah's last messenger

Sunna or Sunnah the book outlining Mohammad's practices and teachings

taqwa a person's consciousness of Allah

Tawaf religious rite performed by Hajj pilgrims; walking around the Kaaba seven times

Um Ali Egyptian sweet made from puff pastry, pistachio nuts, sugar, milk and cream

Umrah out-of-Hajj-season pilgrimage to Mecca

Warak enab vine leaves stuffed with rice and mince (also known as dolma or dolmades)

za'atar oregano herb, spice and seed mixture

zakat Fourth Pillar of Islam; to give charity; system of charity

Zamzam water well located in Mecca; believed to have been miraculously generated and of unending supply

Acknowledgements

I would like to start by thanking Allah the most merciful and benevolent, for giving me the chance to write this book. I thank him for his countless blessings in my life.

To my dear parents, Hatem and Asmaa, I thank you for all you have done for me. Your continuing love and support is something I can never live without. To my dear sisters, Maha and Reem, thank you for allowing me to tell some of your life in this book. May Allah grant you the best of what you want in life and the hereafter. My dear brothers, Firas and Mohammad, I am so proud of what you have achieved in life and your love is always within me.

To my dear husband and friend Hazem, my love and respect for you grows each day. You are truly my soul mate.

My three bundles of joy, Lamya, Zayd and Serene. I hope one day you will grow to see just how much you mean to me. To my extended family and Hazem's family, life without you is just not the same. May happiness always be a part of our lives.

To all the friends who have lent me an ear during the writing of this book, your support and critique is something I couldn't have gone without. To everyone who has been mentioned in this book I hope I have done your mention justice and may it be for you a source of *sadaqa* in the afterlife.

Thank you to everyone at Hachette Australia, including Fiona Hazard, Anne Macpherson, Jessica Luca, Karen Ward, Roberta Ivers, Belinda Lee, Deonie Fiford, Matt Richell and Brendan Fredericks.

Thank you also Christa Moffitt, of Christabella Designs, for the beautiful cover.

To Andrew Fraser and Vanessa Radnidge, thank you for your ongoing friendship through my journey in writing this book.

Form "J"

Government of Palestine

Certificate of Registration

Application No. ....

Deed No. ....

Land Registry Office of ....

Volume No. ....

Folio No. ....

District	Sub-District	Town or Village	Block		Parcel No.
			No.	Name	Reference to Map Sheet No.

					Remarks
Category of Property					
Area	Dunums	Metres		Decimetres	
Share					
Mukta'a					
Name of Former Owner					
Nature of Transaction					
Consideration or Price					

The property above described is registered in the name of ....

of .... and this Certificate is delivered to him as a Certificate of such Registration.

This Certificate of Registration is issued under the Land Settlement Ordinance, 1928.

Date ....

Seal of Land Registry Office.

Registrar of Lands.

When my dad received his father's papers after his death there were deeds to land his family had owned in Palestine. Even all these years later, the pain of having to leave his home and find a new place to live resonates deeply.

He and my mother brought us to Australia so we would have a place to call our home and never have to experience what they did.

If you would like to find out more about
Hachette Australia, our authors, upcoming events
and new releases you can visit our website or
follow us on twitter.

www.hachette.com.au
www.twitter.com/HachetteAus

Arwa El Masri's management can be contacted via
teawitharwa@hotmail.com

www.ingramcontent.com/pod-product-compliance
Ingram Content Group UK Ltd.
Pitfield, Milton Keynes, MK11 3LW, UK
UKHW041300180426
11947UKWH00009B/585

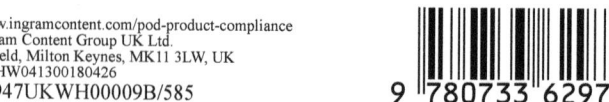